THE CURRENT
ANTIQUE FURNITURE
STYLE & PRICE GUIDE

Other Books by the Same Author

FROM GUNK TO GLOW

THE FURNITURE DOCTOR

THE NEW ANTIQUES

ANTIQUES YOU CAN DECORATE WITH

INSTANT FURNITURE REFINISHING

STAINING AND REFINISHING UNFINISHED FURNITURE
    AND OTHER NAKED WOODS

DECORATING FURNITURE WITH A LITTLE BIT OF CLASS

THE ANTIQUE RESTORER'S HANDBOOK

THE FUN OF REFINISHING FURNITURE

THE CURRENT
ANTIQUE FURNITURE
STYLE & PRICE GUIDE

With Decorative Accessories

Edited by GEORGE GROTZ

DOUBLEDAY & COMPANY, INC., GARDEN CITY, NEW YORK

ACKNOWLEDGMENTS

The editor and publisher are deeply indebted to the following for their help in preparing this guide:

Leonard's Antiques, Route 44, Seekonk, Massachusetts. R. F. Jenkins and J. B. Jenkins, Proprietors.

Morton's Auction Exchange, 643 Magazine Street, New Orleans, Louisiana.

The Wilson Galleries, Fort Defiance, Virginia. Dean and Mark Wilson, Proprietors.

Library of Congress Cataloging in Publication Data

Grotz, George.
The current antique furniture style & price guide.

1. Furniture—England—Catalogs. 2. Furniture
—France—Catalogs. 3. Furniture—United States—
Catalogs. I. Title.
NK2547.G7   749.2
ISBN: 0-385-13165-8
Library of Congress Catalog Card Number 77–27673

CONTENTS

PREFACE

For Whom the Gavel Bangs

This is the first edition of *The Current Antique Furniture Style & Price Guide*. In it we have endeavored to cover the mainstream of popular English, French, and American antiques that are commonly used in interior decoration.

The Golden Century

We are primarily interested in the English, French, and American furniture styles of the 1700s and on into the early 1800s. This period is often referred to as The Golden Century of Furniture Design, because it was during this period that furniture design became a popular art, expressing the changing moods of the people and the exuberant spirit of the times.

The roots of this phenomenon were economic and social. What happened was that the mercantile expansion of England and France created a new middle class—between the nobility and the peasants—that could afford furniture. A new need had come into being, and it was soon met by designers and craft shops of amazing productivity that catered to the popular taste.

The result was the development of a number of definite styles—in spite of a great deal of overlapping—which produced many transitional pieces. In England these styles were Queen Anne, Chippendale, Adam, Hepplewhite, Sheraton, and Regency. Plus English Windsor chairs. In France the styles were Louis XIV, Louis XV, Louis XVI, Directoire, Consulate, Empire, and Provincial (a simplified version of Louis XV). All these styles were then reflected in America in one way or another.

The way this happened was that, after Queen Anne, all the English styles were influenced by whatever was going on in France, and the English results were copied in America. This went on until the end of the eighteenth century, when Empire came directly to the United States as a result of our new closeness to France after the Revolution.

Duplicate Terminology

Because so many transitional pieces were produced, we are including a style guide to the various designs and decorative motifs to help the reader identify any given piece. Our captions in the following pages are written with reference to this guide. However, the greatest cause of confusion in identifying antiques is duplication of terminology, a problem we have decided to deal with head on. Whenever possible, we have chosen to identify the style of a piece by the name of the designer associated with it, as opposed to using the name of a ruler of a country or of a historical period. Some of the difficulties this helps us to overcome—as also illustrated in our style guide—are as follows:

In American furniture the main problem is the use of the term "Federal" to indicate furniture made in the United States after 1776. But there is actually no such style in terms of design (excepting the use of an eagle as decoration). The truth is that Federal furniture is a veritable *pot pourri* of design ideas taken from the styles of Adam, Hepplewhite, Sheraton, and Empire.

A related problem is the use of the term "Duncan Phyfe" as a descriptive of a style. Phyfe was simply one of the leading producers of Federal furniture—in which he happened to combine superbly the styles mentioned above. Some of his later pieces, however, were excellent examples of American Empire, a simplification of the French version to accommodate the American bandsaw.

Moving over to England, we find similar confusion, arising from the English penchant for invoking the names of royalty whenever possible. Englishmen simply can't help themselves when it comes to using the terms George I, George II, and George III for styles of furniture popular during the reigns of these three kings.

To use these terms in England is certainly an Englishman's right. We are all entitled to take pride in our national institutions. It seems to this observer, however, to be a different matter in the United States. To refer to what is obviously a Chippendale chair as George II, or even simply Georgian, does seem to smack of "effete intellectual snobbism"—or at least an insecure individual's attempt at one-upmanship.

At any rate, the term "George I" is used by the English to indicate furniture made during the reign of Queen Anne and up until the definite establishment of the Chippendale style in the reign of George II. And since this was a transitional period, a great deal of such furniture looks just like Chippendale. In fact, the ball-and-claw foot from the Orient was already in use. So the confusion is already real enough without adding to it by inexactness and a duplication of terms. If a chair has a Queen Anne back and a Chippendale ball-and-claw foot, why not take note of both features and class it as transitional? As opposed to falling back on the safe obscurantism of calling it George II—or even more obscurely calling it merely Georgian.

In English usage, then, "George I" refers to transitional pieces between the styles of Queen Anne and Chippendale—weighted on the Chippendale side.

In English usage, "George II" refers to pieces in the well-developed Chippendale style as recorded by Mr. Chippendale in his drawing book of furniture designs that are "in the French Manner." "In the French manner" meaning, of course, pretty heavily decorated with ornate, rococo carving.

Finally, in England the term "George III" covers the styles of the classic revival in England: Adam, Hepplewhite, and Sheraton—which makes the term "George III" the most evasive of all.

In the French furniture styles we find less confusion. To be sure, the names of kings are used, but there is no duplicating of them with the names of designers. Of course, furniture in the style of Louis XIV can be *described* as baroque—and Louis XV is definitely what we mean by rococo—with its use of curved lines and graceful ornamentation.

The main problem we run into with French furniture is distinquishing between Directoire and Consulate, for they both are transitional reaches into the classical architectural lines of the Empire style as Napoleon would soon define it by decree.

Reproductions and Centennials

Two other terms used to describe furniture in the following pages deserve further definition.

The first is the term "reproduction." To be sure, the Romans made reproductions of Greek couches, and choir stalls of the twelfth century were reproduced without guile or intended deception in the sixteenth. The practice has always been with us, and seems unlikely to die.

But in our context the term "reproduction" refers to furniture made in the United States since the early 1900s by a relatively few companies catering to the "carriage trade." This is furniture that was made in careful imitation of the English styles of the 1700s. And it was sold for exactly what it was, to families whose "taste" exceeded their financial resources.

Such reproductions often come into the antique marketplace along with authentic antiques when a large estate is sold. They might have been in a summer house or might have been moved to the servants' quarters when finer things became affordable. And since these pieces usually have very good lines and were well constructed, they are still valued for what they are.

There is, of course, no problem in identifying reproductions, because of the machine dovetailing and machine-planing marks that are easily seen on interior surfaces. On the other hand, it is possible that some such pieces have been artfully distressed and are passed off by owners as the real thing—at least to guests who are diffident about turning chairs upside down to inspect the joining or about slyly pulling drawers out a few inches to check the dovetailing.

The other term to be discussed, "Centennial," should be the cause of considerably more concern due to the unusual amount of "antique" English furniture appearing on the American market in recent years. In a famous book called *Good-bye, Mr. Chippendale,* the author speculated that there were secret factories in England where the manufacture of antiques was a major industry. And there are stories of secret places in Manhattan to which you can take a broken-off chair leg on Wednesday morning and get back a whole chair by late Friday afternoon.

9

The truth of the matter is less romantic. And it comes in two parts. The first part is that we think of England as a small island—the prejudice of people who live in a very big country. But England is not really all that small. And it has been densely populated for a long time. Also, the current prices on antique pieces of English furniture tend to give us the impression that they must have come from the houses of aristocracy. But that is not the case. At the time these pieces of furniture were made, anyone who could afford to own a house could afford this kind of furniture to put into it. Not everyone in England, perhaps, but millions of people could.

So there really was a lot of this furniture when it became time, in the 1920s, for the pickers to go to work. It had filled English houses until, say, the middle of the nineteenth century, when the output of the Victorian furniture factories began to be felt. This does not mean that the old furniture was then thrown away, to be replaced by the new Victorian styles. It stayed where it was, and the new Victorian pieces went into the new homes of an expanding population made possible by the industrial revolution.

This brings us to the time of the Centennial pieces and to a less pleasing reason for the plethora of English antique furniture on the market. For, in the half century following 1876, which was *our* Centennial, people in England were also looking fondly into *their* past, and one of the ways they celebrated it was by manufacturing reproductions of Queen Anne and, particularly, Chippendale furniture—especially chairs. They turned out the reproductions with a zeal only early Victorian factory owners possessed.

Here we have a large group of reproductions of early English styles made in England, all of it now approaching the age of a hundred years or more. And if there is any abuse in the antiques business that deserves correcting, it is the failure to identify these pieces correctly. Especially the sets of chairs, for they are the hardest to tell from the originals.

The trouble is that it is not literal misrepresentation to say of such a set of chairs that (1) they are antiques; (2) they are in the Queen Anne style; (3) they are imported from England. When the three sentences are put together, however, they seem to say something that isn't true at all. *Caveat emptor.*

Restoration

Another term that may deserve our consideration is "restoration." Here the main problem is that it is often hard to decide how far to go with restoration, or even if it should be undertaken at all. Generally speaking, the rule is that the older the piece, the less restoration should be done. But in specific cases the rule isn't of much help. How do you determine exactly how bad the finish on a valuable piece must be before you refinish it? And at what point should the end of a worn-off leg be replaced? And should the repair be left obvious by not staining the new wood, or not?

10

The only thing we can be sure of is that in any financial transaction a restoration that is known by the seller to be such should be pointed out to the buyer. This is a matter about which reputable dealers are very careful.

Then, there are the cases where parts of various pieces have been combined. If the parts are of the same vintage, it may take a good detective to determine what has been done, and then a philosopher to decide on the value of the piece.

Probably the commonest occurrence in this area is the "married highboy." The reason we find so many examples is that it was a practice of the descendants of the original owners to separate the sections for utilitarian purposes.

For instance, the top might go upstairs to a bedroom where a chest of drawers was needed, and the bottom might be kept downstairs for a sideboard— or even be demoted to use in the kitchen when modern furniture was bought. Then, when the estate was being settled after a death, the pieces would be sold separately or given to different heirs.

As a result of this sort of thing, many tops and bottoms are found separately and are soon married by perfectly reputable dealers to supply a strong demand for such pieces—which move well in the $1,500 to $2,500 range. At such prices they are probably one of the best investments that can be made today in antique furniture. Because investors in the matched highboys have already pushed prices up to $70,000 for some of them, the married ones will soon be all that is available. Then the pressures of the marketplace will inevitably begin to work on the married pieces.

Method of Pricing

At this point some reflections on the reporting and predicting of antique prices may be in order.

In recent years a great deal of attention has been paid to the method of pricing antiques through the use of a computer. Prices from auction reports and advertisements are punched into the cards, which are then fed to a computer that prints them on an impressive-looking list.

Now, we cannot help having noticed in our own experience that prices obtained at auctions for the same sort of piece can vary drastically— even from early to late in the same auction. Competition between excited bidders can drive the going-gone price of a piece far over what it should be. On the other hand, at a poorly attended auction—or after the major bidders have spent their limit— many a small bidder gets a lucky break. That is what auctions are all about.

As to the prices seen in advertisements, these can range from a low price set by a dealer in a fit of depression to a price so high that one can only speculate that the seller has recently acquired an opium pipe.

We were confirmed in our suspicion of the efficiency of computer pricing when a young man from I.B.M. told us that the first rule you learn about computer programing is: "Garbage in, garbage out."

11

Therefore, we decided that the prices given in this guide should be arrived at by old-fashioned human intelligence. They would be prices agreed upon by seasoned dealers who are daily involved in buying and selling the kind of pieces shown in this guide. They are the prices at which these dealers expect to sell these pieces during the next year or so in well-managed shops such as their own.

As to regional differences in prices across the United States, this problem is actually very small for pieces of the quality shown in this guide. That is because there is an established national market for these pieces. The differences that do exist are caused by the additional cost of transportation from the East Coast to the West Coast, say, or by the higher cost of shipping containers from England to Gulf Coast and West Coast ports. The prices given in this guide are those prevalent in shops east of the Mississippi River.

The Current Turkey-Shoot

Finally, perhaps something should be said about the prices currently being paid at the top of the market. By this I mean the prices being paid by famous antique stores at auctions run by the leading galleries in London and New York. As an example, consider the $154,000 paid last year by the firm of Israel Sack at Christie's Americana Sale for a blockfront kneehole desk—and $175,000 for two Queen Anne chairs.

Such prices may sound like something out of Alice in Wonderland, but they are not. They are really just part of an old-fashioned turkey-shoot—stimulated by the arrival in the last few years of the new variety of Arabian turkeys. Not that I mean to infer any actual conspiracy on the part of the firms that have been bidding these pieces up. It is simply the same kind of fun that the stockbrokers on Wall Street were having in the 1920's. The higher the prices, the bigger the commissions.

And if you think that the relative value of all art and antiques must always go up, not so. That myth has the same basis as all superstitions: we remember the names of the winners, because they are still around, while the names of the loosers are soon forgotten.

Crystal Ball Department

However, in any market—booming or not—there are always sleepers as well as sucker stocks. For instance, at the same sale mentioned above, two parlor pieces attributed to Belter went for as low as $2,600 and $3,800, which is pretty amazing when you consider: (1) their basic scarcity, (2) the prohibitive cost of faking such pieces—bent rosewood plywood, indeed! and (3) above all, the fact that we are just beginning to appreciate them as part of our cultural heritage.

For it is the "roots" factor we must always remember in looking for the sleepers. After all, the basic value of all antiques is that they tell us who we were—as we become ready to appreciate each wave of the past that overtakes us.

Which brings us to the biggest sleeper of them all in today's market: the "married" highboy that can still be picked up in the $1,500 range. Here again, the hidden value lies in the cultural heritage factor: the story of how the original pieces got divorced and a new marriage was made. And you can't get any more American than divorces and remarriages. It's the best conversation piece to come down the pike for many a year.

So that's all for this time. Until next time, ask not for whom the gavel bangs—it bangs for you.

Good Hunting!

George Grotz

STYLE GUIDE

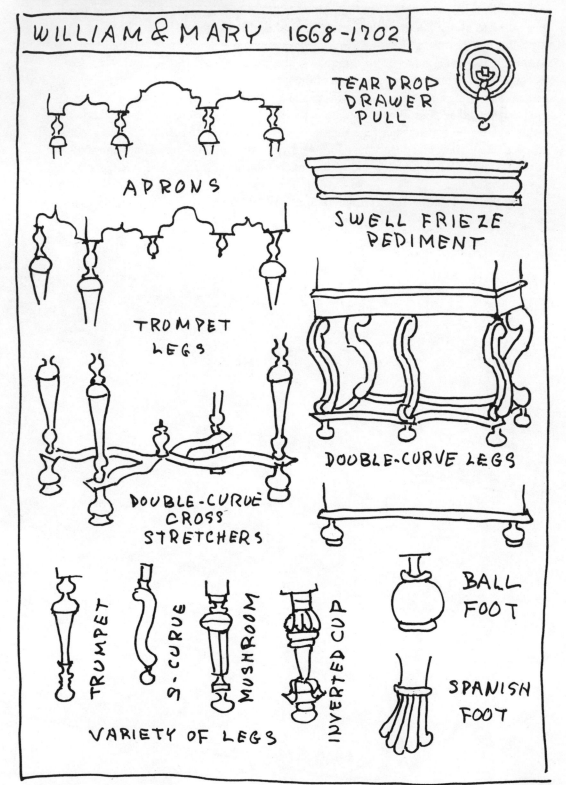

WILLIAM & MARY 1668-1702

APRONS

TEAR DROP DRAWER PULL

SWELL FRIEZE PEDIMENT

TROMPET LEGS

DOUBLE-CURVE CROSS STRETCHERS

DOUBLE-CURVE LEGS

TRUMPET S-CURVE MUSHROOM INVERTED CUP

VARIETY OF LEGS

BALL FOOT

SPANISH FOOT

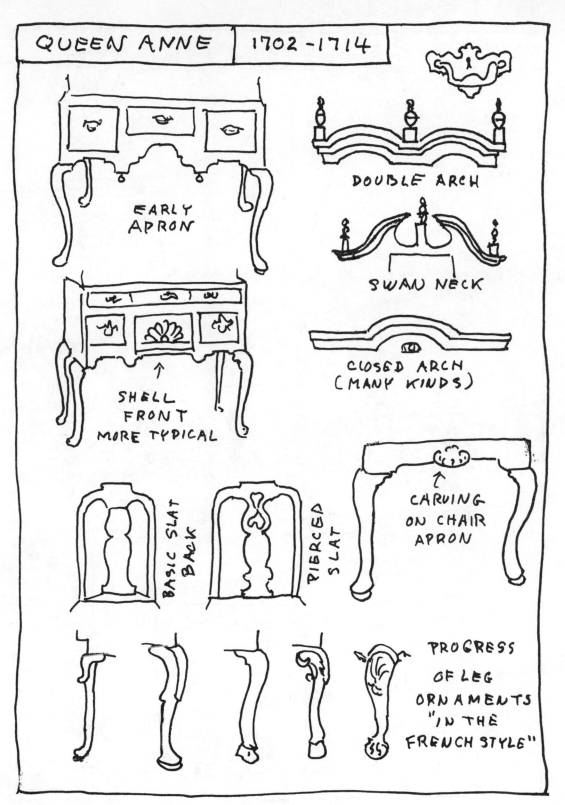

QUEEN ANNE | 1702-1714

EARLY APRON

SHELL FRONT MORE TYPICAL

DOUBLE ARCH

SWAN NECK

CLOSED ARCH (MANY KINDS)

BASIC SLAT BACK

PIERCED SLAT

CARVING ON CHAIR APRON

PROGRESS OF LEG ORNAMENTS "IN THE FRENCH STYLE"

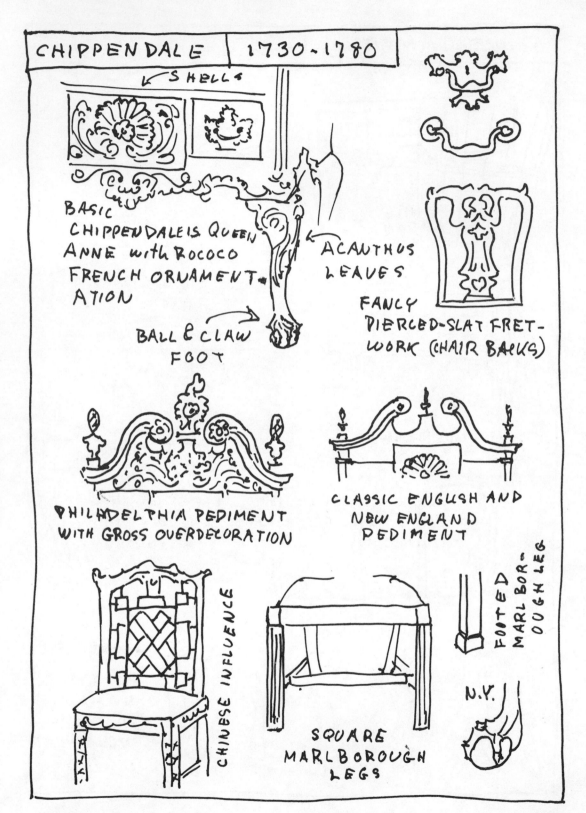

CHIPPENDALE | 1730-1780

SHELLS

BASIC CHIPPENDALE IS QUEEN ANNE WITH ROCOCO FRENCH ORNAMENTATION

BALL & CLAW FOOT

ACANTHUS LEAVES

FANCY PIERCED-SLAT FRETWORK (CHAIR BACKS)

PHILADELPHIA PEDIMENT WITH GROSS OVERDECORATION

CLASSIC ENGLISH AND NEW ENGLAND PEDIMENT

CHINESE INFLUENCE

SQUARE MARLBOROUGH LEGS

FOOTED MARLBOROUGH LEG

N.Y.

WINDSOR CHAIRS | 1725-1825

BASIC BOW BACK
WINDSOR

HEAVIER
ORIGINAL
ENGLISH
STYLE

FAN
BACK

BIRD-
CAGE

CONTINUOUS
ARM

ADAM BROS. 1758 - 1792

AN ARCHITECT'S ODD CONCEIT THAT ENGLISH FURNITURE SHOULD LOOK LIKE ROMAN BUILDINGS

HEPPLEWHITE ?-1786

A MAJOR
STYLE
EVOLVED
FROM
ADAM
STYLE

19

SHERATON | 1790-1806

ROUND BRASS KNOBS

"ROMAN" SWAG CARVING

LYRE BACK

MOSTLY REEDED LEGS

BRASS FEET & CASTERS

ON TABLES

COOKIE-TOP LEG

REGENCY (ENG.) | 1793-1820

ENGLAND'S SINCEREST
FORM OF FLATTERY FOR
FRANCE'S EMPIRE STYLE

SPHINXES
AND SUCH

BRASS
SCREENING

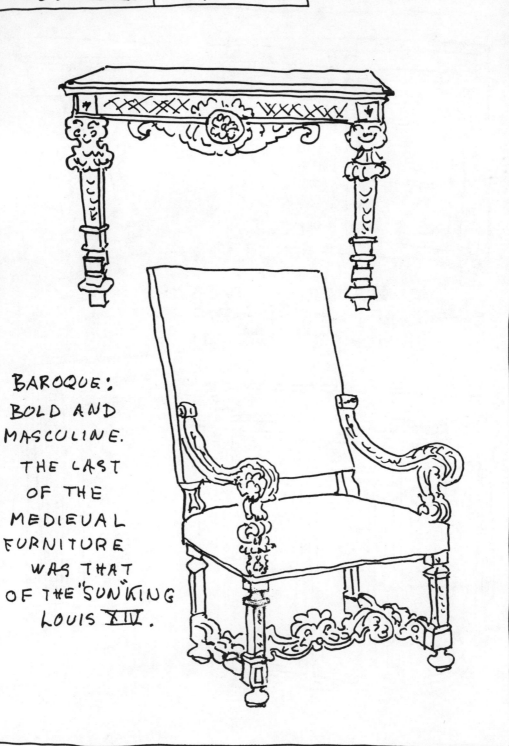

BAROQUE:
BOLD AND
MASCULINE.
THE LAST
OF THE
MEDIEVAL
FURNITURE
WAS THAT
OF THE "SUN KING"
LOUIS XIV.

LOUIS XV | 1715-1774

WITH ROCOCO
THE CURVED
LINE REIGNED
SUPREME

PROVINCIAL | 1730 —

SIMPLIFIED
"COUNTRY"-MADE
LOUIS XV
BECAME A
BASIC STYLE

24

LOUIS XVI | 1774-1793

A CLASSIC
REVIVAL
WITH
HINTS OF
THE EMPIRE
STYLE
TO COME

DIRECTOIRE-
CONSULATE

1795-1804

9 YEARS OF
TRANSITION
FROM LOUIS XVI
TO EMPIRE

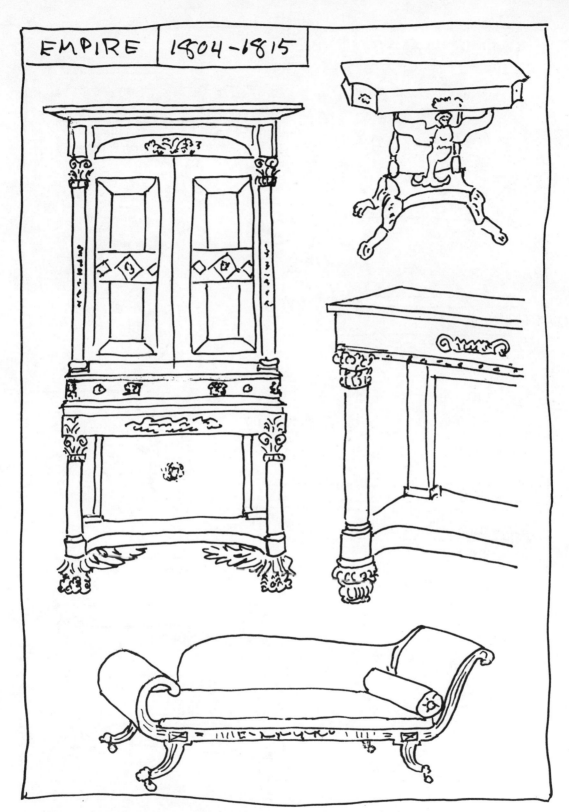

EMPIRE 1804-1815

AMERICAN EMPIRE

FEDERAL
VERSION →
(1790-1850)

WINGED
CLAW
FEET

PILLAR & SCROLL
(1850-1900)

28

GLOSSARY

acanthus leaf – An herbaceous plant or weed commonly found on the Greek peninsula and over into Asia Minor. Its shape was used by ancient Greeks and Romans to decorate their furniture and buildings. The tops of Corinthian columns are in the shape of nicely arranged acanthus leaves. From about 1715 to 1760—as recorded by Thomas Chippendale—they were all the rage in England.

Adam – A style of furniture designed and made under the direction of the two Adam brothers, who were also architects and interior designers and decorators. The older brother, Robert, brought the classical inspiration for their designs back from Italy, where he had observed the excavation of an ancient Roman city—Herculaneum.

armoire – A cupboard with two full-length doors that is used for hanging clothes. If it has shelves inside, it is called a linen press.

Aubusson – Tapestries woven in the French village of the same name. Also reasonable facsimiles and imitations. Appearing on upholstered pieces of the Louis XV and Louis XVI styles.

bachelor's chest – Generally speaking, any small four-drawer chest in the English styles of the eighteenth century. More properly, the top drawer should be divided into two separate drawers.

bail – The hanging handle of a drawer pull.

baroque – If rococo was graceful and feminine, baroque was bold and masculine. Baroque was the style of the 1600s and the enthusiastic Renaissance of Europe. It consisted of extra-large and gross overdecoration, all gilded and painted in brilliant colors. With inlays, marquetry and boulle, marble and metals, they went about as far as you could go in the seventeenth century.

Belter – John Henry Belter was a New York City cabinetmaker, circa 1850, noted for finely carved furniture of laminated rosewood in a rococo manner. Also worked in other styles of the American Empire period.

bergère – A low-backed armchair with elbow arms closed or filled in with upholstery. The term is used for both the whole chair and the arm itself (as opposed to the *fauteuil* chair or arm, in which the space inside the arm is left open).

bibliothèque – French for bookcase.

Biedermeier – The French Empire style as it was rather closely copied in Germany.

bonheur du jour – A small and usually square-topped *bureau-plat* or writing table. Also used as a dressing or primping table.

boulle – Inlay work in which brass has been laid into wood or tortoise shell. This work is named after the ebonist who invented the process in Paris in the era of Louis XIV. Also strangely spelled "buhl" by the English.

bureau – In America, a high chest of drawers for use in a bedroom. (See *dresser*.) In England, any kind of desk, including slant-fronts. Although it is an English word, the plural in both countries is *bureaux,* though in the United States *bureaus* is permissible.

bureau-bookcase – The English term for a secretary.

bureau-plat – French word for writing table. A rectangular, flat-topped table with one or more drawers right under the top.

cabriole leg – The Queen Anne leg. Or any other leg curving out at the top and in at the bottom, as the Louis XV leg. Originated in Italy, where it was supposedly inspired by a goat's hind leg.

camel back – A Hepplewhite sofa with a hump in the back.

canterbury – A Georgian music carrier, now thought of as a magazine rack.

chesterfield – An English overstuffed couch of rectangular shape covered with button-tufted leather.

cheval mirror – A full-length mirror mounted on vertical posts so that it can tilt forward and back.

chiffonier – An English word since about 1860, from the French word of the same spelling. Being in either language: a small cupboard with drawers for odds and ends, not so high that the top cannot be used as a sideboard. (An indefinite word, indefinitely used.)

chinoiserie – Anything in the Chinese manner—whether a piece of furniture, a design, or a decoration.

Chippendale – An English style of furniture arrived at in the first half of the eighteenth century by applying carved decoration "in the French manner" to the basic English style called Queen Anne. (See *rococo*.)

Chippendale, Thomas – A successful cabinetmaker of the mid-eighteenth century. In 1754 he published a book of the popular designs of the time called *The Gentleman and Cabinet-Makers Director,* to which the subtitle for the first edition read: "to Furniture in the French Taste." (See *rococo*.)

commode – A low chest having two doors under a single drawer.

consul table – A table that mounts against the wall.

Coromandel – Strictly speaking, an ebony-like wood from the coast of India. But also a black lacquer imitating it that was used as a base for incised and painted screens, some of which date back to the early 1700s. Their manufacture has been uninterrupted since then.

credenza – A sideboard with two doors in front that are usually under a drawer placed right under the top. Same as a commode, only much larger—three to four feet high.

cupboard – A chest piece with doors on the front, and sometimes a row of drawers (or one drawer above the doors or door). Also the same sort of chest with set-back shelves on top of it, also closed by one or two doors, but not necessarily so. Usually intended to contain and/or display china, pewter, or other eating utensils. (See *dresser*.)

davenport – In England, a small writing desk of the mid-Victorian Era—with a lift-top and drawers in one or both sides. It was named for its manufacturer. In the United States, a davenport is variously an upholstered sofa or an upholstered couch that can be unfolded to make a bed.

dresser – In America, a low chest of drawers with a mirror mounted on the back of it, usually tilting. In England, a large cupboard without doors. Usually called a Welsh dresser if it has simple country lines.

ebonist – (From the French *ébéniste*) One who works in ebony, a very hard and difficult wood to use. By extension, a French cabinetmaker.

Empire – In no other time in history has a style of furniture so clearly expressed an idea of its country's meaning and purpose—in this case Napoleon's idea of an Empire modeled after the Roman Empire. Simple, massive, dignified, imperial, honest. It was an idea with broad appeal—while it lasted.

étagère – A set of free-standing shelves first found in the styles of Louis XVI and Sheraton. Simple and restrained in the French manner, these pieces evolved into the fussy, fretwork whatnots of the mid-Victorian Era—for which the term *étagère* was often retained.

fauteuil – An upholstered French armchair with open elbow arms (as opposed to the closed-arm style, which is called *bergère*).

fluting – Vertical grooves of the kind seen on Greek and Roman columns.

French foot – A short Hepplewhite leg, as on a chest of drawers, that sweeps slightly outward.

gesso – Plaster of paris mixed with glue, which is applied to a wood surface to prepare it for gilding with bronze powders or gold-leaf, because it can be sanded smoother than wood.

girandole – A convex mirror of the kind ubiquitous to the American Federal period. In French usage, a multiple-socket candleholder.

Gothic – Anything with pointed arches. Like the cathedral at Chartres, for instance.

Governor Winthrop desk – A slant-front desk in the American style of simplified Chippendale. Because Governor Winthrop had one.

Hepplewhite – Two years after his death in 1786, George Hepplewhite's wife, Alice, published a book of designs that he had collected of the popular work of his period. They were also designs he had used in his own shop. They all showed the strong influence of the Adam designs that inspired them, and were even improved by the need to make those designs more functional to attract customers in a competitive market.

hutch – Originally a simple Jacobean sideboard, but now an Early American-style chair with a round back that folds down onto the arms to make a table. There is also usually a storage box under the hinged seat.

inlay – Decorative designs made of pieces of veneer, tortoise shell, mother-of-pearl, and other materials set flush into a wood surface.

Jacobean – Strictly speaking, the term applies to furniture made in the reigns of James I and James II in England—that is, from around 1600 to 1660. But because it isn't much different, it also applies to furniture actually made in the preceding reign of Queen Elizabeth.

kas – Pennsylvania Dutch word for wardrobe, properly on ball feet.

Kauffmann, Angelica – The usual phrase is "panels painted in the manner of Angelica Kauffmann." Working with the Adam brothers, as architects, she painted ceilings, walls, and furniture with classical designs. Her work was also widely copied on furniture in the Adam, Hepplewhite, and Sheraton styles.

kingwood – Very similar to rosewood, and used in fine French furniture.

linen press – Originally a device used for pressing linen between two boards, often built into cupboards. Now used as a term for a wardrobe that is full of shelves—i.e., clothes cannot be hung in it, but linens can be stored in it.

Louis XIV – Under the reign of Louis XIV, France finally emerged from the Medieval Age with its domination by royal families and the Church. Like England, France became a bustling mercantile and trading nation. So the French called their ruler The Sun King, and celebrated themselves with baroque overdecoration of their furniture, among other things. During these decades the economic foundation was laid for the cultural explosion in the era of . . .

Louis XV – As France continued to prosper in the first half of the eighteenth century, the art of furniture design reached one of its peaks in the rococo style. For the first time, furniture design rejected the squares and rectangles of architecture to follow the curving lines of nature (as in *art nouveau* and Frank Lloyd Wright!). The lightest and most graceful of furniture designs, Louis XV is universally considered to be the quintessence of the French spirit.

Louis XVI – In the eighteenth century, when Europe was still newly out of the Medieval Age, even the French could not resist the classic revival that resulted from the excavation of Greek and Roman ruins. But they certainly gave the classical lines a distinctly French flavor—which is more than can be said for Adam and Hepplewhite.

Marlborough leg – The square Chippendale leg without a foot.

marquetry – A whole surface covered with pieces of veneer of various woods to form a pattern. Decorative designs are then usually laid flush into this background. The best examples are seen in the period of Louis XV.

ogee – A double curve. As commonly seen in American Empire veneered mirror frames and the carved Chippendale block foot.

ormolu – Brass castings used to decorate French furniture. They were originally gold-leafed.

patina – The "old" look of a wood surface, finished or not—widely believed to be impossible for the forger to reproduce. Actually, it is quite easy for any competent finisher to duplicate, and he is usually does.

pembroke table – A small drop-leaf table whose top is wider than its leaves.

pillar and scroll – A term used to describe clock cases by Eli Terry and others of the period. Also used for American Empire furniture of the later period— i.e., as simplified for mass production. From which also comes the term "bandsaw" Empire.

Queen Anne – A work of art is a man alive, but no one knows who was the first man to carve the quiet beauty of the Queen Anne cabriole leg. So we call it by the name of the ruler under whom it was created during the cultural excitement in England that followed the expulsion of the foreigners William and Mary.

rococo – Designs that followed the curving lines of nature not only in decoration, but also in structural members; in furniture, the style of Louis XV and Provincial. Once popular in France, the style was then applied to the English style of Queen Anne to arrive at the style called Chippendale.

secretary – Any desk with bookshelves built on top of it. (Usually a slant-front desk, but not necessarily so.)

semainier – A French word for a narrow chest of about shoulder height, which contains seven drawers, stemming from the fact that the French word for week is *semaine*. Occasionally a semainier will contain only six drawers—for people who sleep all day Sunday. Also, sometimes, with eight drawers, which must be for some strange French reason.

Sèvres plaques – Hand-painted porcelain pieces used to decorate furniture. Used discreetly on Louis XV furniture, but with wild abandon on Louis XVI pieces.

Sheraton – Like Chippendale and Hepplewhite, Thomas Sheraton also assembled examples of the popular styles of his time in various publications. In fact, his drawing book is believed to have been used by five or six hundred cabinet shops in England. What his designs reflect, of course, is the influence of French styles on the current English classicism.

sideboard – Any flat-topped chest with drawers or door-enclosed spaces useful for storing utensils, silverware, and linens used in serving meals—serving dishes being placed on top of it during the serving process. They are most familiar to us in the styles of Hepplewhite and Sheraton.

Sutherland table – English term for a narrow (when closed) gate-leg table.

vernis martin Picture panels on furniture done in lacquers. Seen on furniture of the Louis XIV and Louis XV styles.

Welsh dresser – A comparatively wide sideboard having only one level of drawers and a set-back set of open shelves on the top—i.e., no doors in front of the shelves, as a cupboard has.

33

BEDS

Maple rope bed of the early 1800s
with ball-and-urn turnings of
exceptional quality. As found . . .
$850

Spool-turned pine bed of the
mid-1800s. As found . . .
$350

Typical Early American
cannonball four-poster from
1800–30. Originally had rope
mattress support. Refinished and
widened for standard mattress.
$650

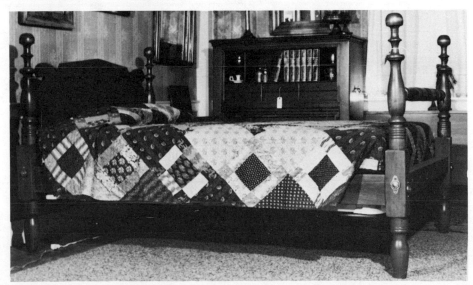

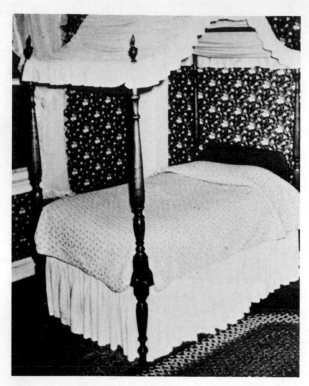

Early American maple child's tester bed. Often called field bed because of tent-shaped top. Circa 1820. Sheraton turnings.
$1,500

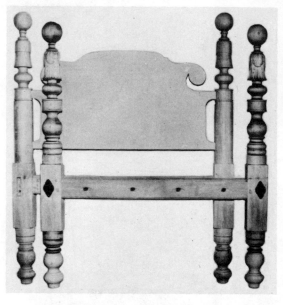

American four-poster of early 1800s with hand-carved bell beneath cannonballs. Fully restored.
$800

Sheraton field tester bed, circa 1820, with pineapple carved posts of the American style. Restored for standard mattress. Rope holes, brass bolt covers.
$2,500

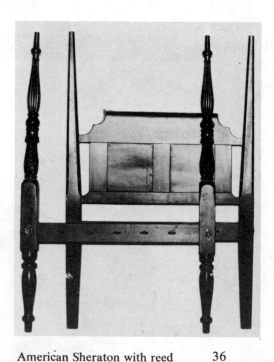

American Sheraton with reed carving on foot posts, octagonal pencil posts with paneled headboard.
$2,000

Maple turnip-top four-poster with turnings on all posts slightly different. Widened and restored.
$675

Acorn four-poster with roll top on headboard and acorn-top posts. Widened and restored.
$600

American tulip-top four-poster in maple with blanket-roll stretcher on feet, pegs for rope mattress net.
$750

American maple four-poster with the simple turnings produced by an apprentice to the lathe. With flat-topped Queen Anne-style headboard. Early 1800s. Widened and restored.
$625

American Empire four-poster, circa 1810 or earlier. Has the elegance of French Empire, with American pineapple in bloom on top of posts. Paneled headboard. Widened.
$950

American four-poster with Queen Anne flat-top headboard and apprentice-turned posts. Refinished and widened.
$700

American brass bed with bowed footboard, circa early 1900s.
$850

Spool turning with pine-tree top, maple, circa 1830. Restored bed . . .
   $600

Popular cannonball and bell turning, maple, circa 1840. As fully restored bed . . .
   $750

Common variation of cannonball and bell with turned foot posts but plain head posts. As fully restored bed . . .
   $750

Urn top, maple, early 1800s. As restored bed . . .
   $650

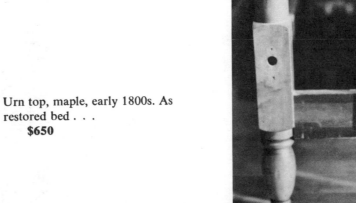

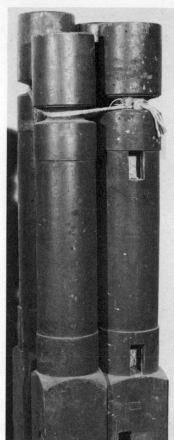

Commonest style of drum-top turning, circa 1790–1810, in maple. As fully restored bed . . .
$600

Early New England style of drum head. Maple with original pinkish milk paint. As fully restored bed with paint preserved . . .
$750

Pineapple on bell, maple, 1830s. As fully restored bed . . .
$800

Elegant hand-carved pineapple on drum, maple, circa 1830. As fully restored bed . . .
$800

Mahogany posts topped by cannonball, drum, and carved bell, circa 1840. As fully restored bed . . .
$950

Cannonball with carved bell on foot posts. As fully restored bed . . .
$900

American Empire field tester bed with acorn top and acanthus-leaf carving on posts.
$1,800

Posts with re-turned tops, but hand-carved twists. As fully restored bed . . .
$900

American tester bed, circa 1820, well-carved, solid mahogany, regal Empire style.
$1,800

American Empire bed in solid mahogany with pineapple carving on top of four posts, 1830. New York origin.
$2,100

Similar American Empire bed combining pineapple and acanthus-leaf carving, 1820.
$1,600

Bedroom Suites, etc.

Victorian Renaissance-style bed, circa mid-1800s. Solid walnut with glued-on walnut carving.
$1,400

Early American Empire bed from the Deep South. Solid and veneer mahogany combined, circa 1840.
$3,200

Early American Empire bed of southern origin. Very French Empire, but made in U.S., dark mahogany, circa 1830.
$3,200

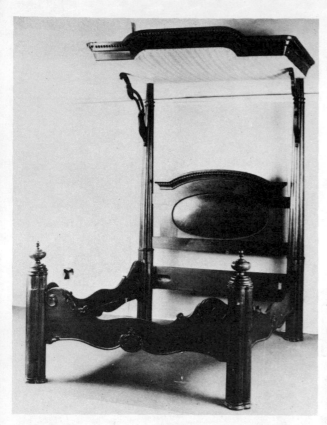

Early American Empire bed. A transitional piece as footboard and posts move into Victorian Renaissance style. Circa 1860.
$2,800

Transitional American Empire into Victorian Renaissance bed. Walnut carving glued onto solid walnut.
$2,600

American bed with reeded posts, in the Sheraton manner. Brass urn finials, headboard of flame-grain mahogany, posts also mahogany. From New York area, circa 1800.
$1,700

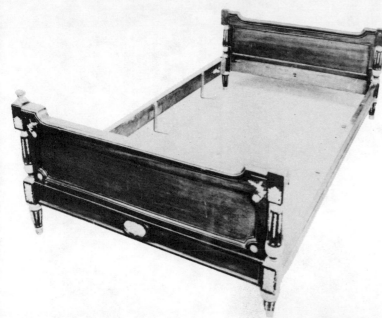

French Louis XVI daybed of solid mahogany with gilded bronze ornamentation called ormolu.
$2,800

Jacobean-style cradle or baby bed of carved walnut in style of 1680s. Made in Victorian Era.
$1,400

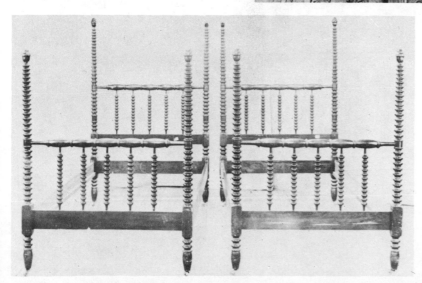

Pair of Early American spool beds from New England or Pennsylvania in maple. Early 1700s.
$2,000

American Depression-style
bedroom set combining elements of
Louis XV with Chippendale
ball-and-claw feet. Made between
1910 and 1930. Mahogany. A
statement about American culture
of the era.
    $1,600

Painted Venetian-style bed.
In style of early 1800s.
    $1,600

Satinwood bedroom set with two
beds, two chests, and dressing
table. A Depression set that this
time combines some French curves
with Hepplewhite ovals. For the
speculative collector.
    $2,200

Lower-priced version of early
Victorian Renaissance-style
bedroom set, 1850–80. Original
false graining and decoration in
excellent condition.
    $600

BOOKCASES

Painted satinwood bookcase in the
Adam manner, made circa 1850.
$1,600

Louis XV marquetry kingwood
bibliothèque, made about 1870.
$1,800

Revolving mahogany bookmill
made in England, circa 1860.
$450

English dwarf bookcase made of
walnut, circa 1890, in an attempt
at Queen Anne style.
$1,250

Three-section American Empire
bookcase with paw feet.
Mahogany.
$2,400

English bookcase-chest with
false-drawer fronts on two bottom
drawers. Mid-1700s, Chippendale
style.
$1,800

American Empire bookcase-cabinet
in mahogany veneer on pine.
$1,400

Empire bookcase with Gothic
beehive arches, circa 1850.
Mahogany.
$1,100

49

French Empire ormolu mounted
double bookcase in mahogany.
$2,200

French Empire ebonized bookcase,
ormolu mounted with porcelain
plaques, circa 1840.
$650

Double-door French ebonized
bookcase with ormolu and boulle
ornamentation of tortoise shell and
brass. Style of Second Empire,
1840–60. Black marble top.
$1,300

50

French Provincial *bibliothèque*
(shelves inside). Nice cabriole legs,
walnut.
     $1,200

Continental bookcase-chest made
of mahogany, circa 1810.
     $1,600

BOXES

Oak Bible box commonly brought over from England. Thirty inches wide, original oil finish.
   $425

Common pine deed box, twenty-four inches wide, flush handles and lock of wrought iron, circa 1830s.
   $85

Victorian letter box with fancy veneering and inlays, fourteen inches wide.
   $125

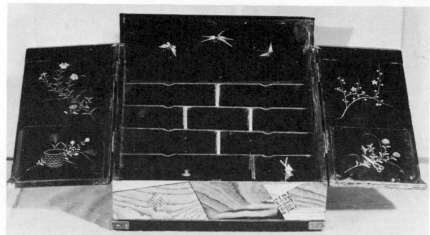

Same box open to show black lacquer work inside.

Pine deed box, twenty inches wide, late 1700s, no handles.
$75

Sea captain's liquor chest of oak with wrought-iron bindings and perfect, complete set of stoppered bottles inside. See next photo.
$550

Inside of sea captain's liquor chest with bottles.

Lap desks for traveling and visiting, full of inkwells and secret compartments.
$100–$300

Pair of fitted English knife boxes of mahogany with satinwood inlays, rosewood banding. Since they have original fittings, which is very rare . . .
$1,800

Single English knife box of same quality as preceding pair.
$450

French traveling box, early 1800s, with mother-of-pearl and brass inlay on top, mostly walnut.
$300

Sèvres porcelain box, circa 1880, painted and signed by the artist.
$475

Miniature chest used as a jewel
box, early 1800s.
$210

Miniature chest used as jewel box.
From mid-1700s with nice metal
pulls.
$350

BREAKFRONTS

Custom-made (circa 1920) Chippendale breakfront in flame mahogany.
$3,200

Authentic Chippendale breakfront with very simple lines. Flame-grain mahogany.
$6,000

Fine broken arch with fretwork tops this authentic Chippendale breakfront. Delicate latticework. 1780s.
$11,000

English burl-walnut breakfront
made 1860–70 in the Queen
Anne manner.
$2,500

Chippendale breakfront with
curled broken-arch pediment in
very dark mahogany.
$7,500

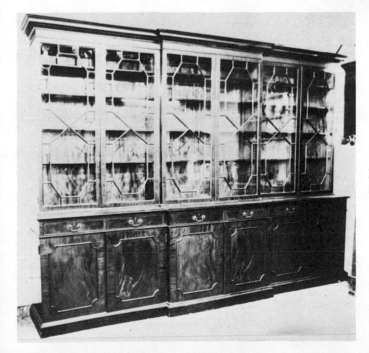

Large three-section breakfront in
mahogany and Chippendale style.
$7,200

Chippendale secretary-breakfront
in mahogany, circa 1760.
   $16,500

Fine Chippendale breakfront with
broken-arch pediment. Excellent
color and grain mahogany.
Compact size pushes its value up,
to . . .
   $14,000

Red lacquered English breakfront
with chinoiseries decoration. Circa
1760 and related to the
Chippendale style in design.
   $2,800

Country-made primitive pine
breakfront from England with
elements of Empire and Gothic
design. Late 1800s.
   $2,000

French Empire bookcase of
rosewood with brass inlay, gilded
columns. A fine piece
custom-made, circa 1920, in New
York City.
$2,800

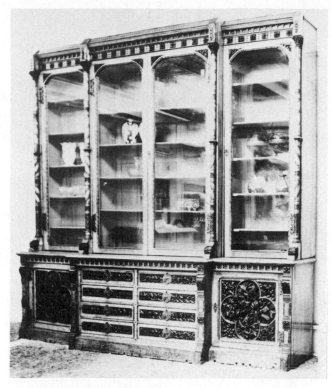

Richly carved oak and walnut
English Victorian breakfront.
$6,500

Unusual French Empire breakfront
of mahogany and satinwood. Fine
Egyptian figures top risers at sides
of doors on bottom. Circa 1810.
$3,600

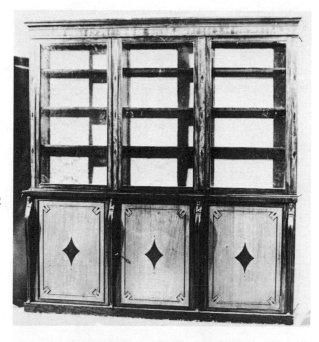

59

CHAIRS

Country-made Queen Anne chair
with yoke back and splint seat.
$450

English Windsor chair with clubby
feet and nonsensical splat.
Victorian reproduction.
$225

American banister-back chair with
scroll top and ball finials.
$450

Country-made chair with Queen Anne back, Spanish feet, and bulbous rail turning. Maple. New England origin.
$750

Banister-back Pilgrim chair from New England, early 1700s. With arms . . .
$1,000

American Windsor chair with seven spindles, New England, circa 1780s. Pine seat and maple legs are bamboo turned.
$300

American bow-back Windsor with heavy pine seat, maple verticals.
$800

Pine and maple high chair, circa 1870s, with heavy, shaped pine back.
$175

New England child's chair in maple, ball finials, circa 1800.
$125

Child's chair from New England, circa 1830–50, in Boston rocker family.
$125

Ballroom chairs were made in large sets, but now are used singly with dressing tables. Original decoration.
$85

Banister-back chair with yoke top
and well-worn extra bulbous
stretcher. Made of maple and oak.
From mid-1600s and often called a
Pilgrim chair.
   $475

Back view of same chair.

Stretcher of same chair.

Bow-back Windsor side chair with characteristically turned leg of 1750 plus spindles (best).
$450

Extra-fine continuous-arm Windsor with comb back for shawl to prevent drafts. Original paint and pop-in joint construction. Mid-1700s.
$2,200

Early Victorian American side
chair with roses and finger carving.
Queen Anne legs.
$125

Close-up of rose carving on
preceding chair.

Early Victorian chair with grapes
and finger carving on Louis XV
legs.
$150

American Empire side chair in solid mahogany and mahogany veneer on mahogany. Fiddleback and saber or curule leg, serpentine curve at front of seat.
$165

Banister-back or Pilgrim chair with crested top reminiscent of Queen Anne, which suggests it dates from late 1600s.
$550

Same chair from behind.

Simple three-slat-back side chair from the late 1600s. Nice finials, but feet well worn off and evened. New seat.
$75

Four-slat-back Pilgrim chair, circa 1700, has arms and mushroom cap on front legs. Old but not original black paint.
$850

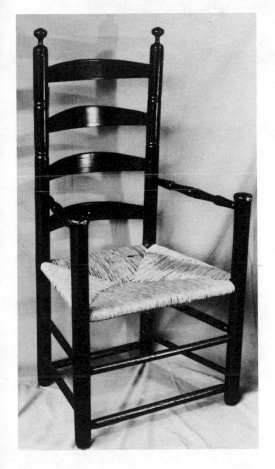

67   Country-made side chair from Pilgrim period, with vase back and curved top of Queen Anne heritage.
$525

Birdcage (or pigeon-coop) Windsor side chairs with usual bamboo turnings. About 1810. For the pair . . .
$350

Heavier, better-made birdcage Windsor chair with bent spindles. Refinished.
$225

Sheraton-style "fancy chair" with arrow-back vertical slats. Remnants of original paint. New seat.
$140

Four slats and heavy finials suggest early 1700s as date for this hoop-skirt armchair. (Arm supports were set back to accommodate hoops.)
$525

Pilgrim yoke-back chair with plain vertical slats, circa 1720–50. Exceptional arms. If feet restored, value is cut in half. With original feet and seat . . .
$1,150

Simple Windsor side chair with bamboo turnings of maple, seat and back top of pine. Scraped.
$125

Note Boston rocker-type arms that put this high chair circa 1820. Rabbit-ear back posts, usual maple and pine construction.
$175

Typical bow-back Windsor chair from mid-1700s. Original paint.
$850

American bow-back Windsor of uncertain "primitive" origin, but old.
$375

"Continental" is the term that dealers fall back on to classify chairs such as these. The style is French-inspired, circa 1700, from somewhere in northern Europe. These were made sometime in the Victorian Era. In a set of eight . . .
$2,400

Good example of Jacobean-style chair (1690) reproduced in Victorian England in oak.
$300

Early English Windsor chair of simple design in oak.
$350

A French Directoire-style side chair with a storage space under the lift-up cane seat. Ormolu mounts, but crude workmanship. Probably circa 1900.
$250

Small Louis XV-style ballroom chair with cabriole legs and scroll feet, needlepoint design, circa 1880.
$400

American early-Victorian prie-dieu in the French influence. Mahogany.
$300

In Belter's early-Victorian style, without ornate carving and in walnut or mahogany, chairs like these are each . . .
$900

Gilded walnut prie-dieu from France in manner of Louis XV. Quite old.
$450

Provincial French-Canadian prie-dieu deeply carved in walnut.
$300

With the carved backs of
laminated rosewood, these two
chairs from left to right are . . .
$1,100 and $1,300

Belter in full bloom. Each of these
chairs is currently worth . . .
$1,600

Set of six English Jacobean-style
dining chairs (two armchairs),
carved oak, circa 1900.
$1,500

Single Jacobean reproduction armchair.
$225

Small spindle-back Yorkshire chair of the mid-1700s.
$350

Jacobean oak folding chairs of the period. Late 1600s. The pair . . .
$1,500

French sedan chair, circa 1760–70, painted green with gold-leafed carving, appropriate hand-painted decoration. Now often used for telephoning or other private matters.
$3,700

Corner

American corner chair from early 1700s. Some pale fruitwood. New rush seat.
$1,200

Chippendale corner chair with Marlborough legs and stretchers. English Victorian origin. Mahogany.
$350

English Victorian reproductions of George I (Queen Anne/Chippendale) corner chairs. As pairs are unusual, for these . . .
$1,000

American Victorian version of an
English corner chair. Inexcusable,
but, since tastes vary . . .
$300

A really mixed-up Georgian corner
chair. Not the most successful
design, but of the period (1770).
$1,100

Dining

Hepplewhite-style shield-back fauteuil armchairs (open arms). Slip-in seats, spade feet. English Victorian reproductions, backs too bold. The pair . . .
    $375

Set of seven chairs in unidentifiable style, but good construction, mahogany, and paw feet.
    $700

Set of six Chippendale ladder backs (ribbon backs). Mahogany. Victorian.
    $2,100

A good example of the sets of
Chippendale chairs produced in
Victorian England. Mahogany.
Design is from the book.
$2,400

Caned Louis XV/Provincial chairs
in fruitwood from late 1700s.
$1,850

Set of Windsor chairs. Six of the
period, five matching Centennials.
$2,400

Set of saber-leg chairs with Queen Anne splat, newly caned seats.
$550

Fancy New England painted chairs in the Sheraton manner with original decoration and rush seats. Set of six . . .
    $1,300

Set of eight, of the period, carved shield-back chairs in the Hepplewhite style. Very authentic. Spade feet. Short arm.
    $6,000

Very plain single Hepplewhite chair, but of the period.
$450

Square-back Hepplewhite, too delicate to be very desirable, but of the period (1780–90), and rather rare due to fragility. Whether single, in pairs, or in sets, for each chair . . .
$450

Set of four authentic Chippendale ladder-back chairs.
$2,500

Classical shield-back Hepplewhite
chair of the period (1790–1800).
Set of four . . .
　　　$2,400

A pair of Chinese teak chairs made
around 1850. Deep curved backs,
low seats, delicate. The pair . . .
　　　$1,200

Pretzel or ladder-back Chippendale
of "Centennial" origin. Mahogany.
　　　$275

Authentic Queen Anne/George I chair.
$850

Chippendale side chair of the period (1760s). Set of six . . .
$4,200

Authentic "of the period" Chippendale chairs. Set of eight . . .
$9,600

Set of eight dining chairs (two armchairs) made in Portugal, circa 1770. Finely carved mahogany. A Portuguese interpretation of Georgian styles. Set of eight . . .
$7,500

82

Pair of highly carved teakwood "palace chairs" from China in the 1860s to England. The pair . . .
   $2,000

Pair of Chinese palace chairs, circa 1860.
   $2,300

Square-back Hepplewhite ballroom chairs with Sheraton legs of uncertain origin, but of the period. Each . . .
   $250

83

Sheraton fancy chairs, circa 1810.
Original paint and decoration.
English origin, fairly rare.
Each . . .
$450

French Directoire chairs of solid
mahogany with heavy veneer
backs. In sets of six or eight, each
chair . . .
$450

French ballroom chairs in walnut.
Directoire style, circa 1800. Of the
period, each . . .
$500

Child's high chair in Sheraton
design. Of the period (1790).
Spade feet.
$450

Satinwood wheel-back chairs with
plaques painted in the manner of
Angelica Kauffmann, circa 1790,
and true Hepplewhite design. For
the pair . . .
$1,500

Victorian-made Queen Anne-style
dining chairs with high, square
backs. Each . . .
$300

A heavy Victorian reproduction chair with strong carving, scroll back, made in 1880 to a 1760 design. Important feeling. Set of four . . .
$2,500

Queen Anne-style chair made in England, circa 1880.
$350

Jacobean-style chairs mass-produced in Victorian England, circa 1890. Set of eight . . .
$2,800

Victorian reproduction oak chairs made in England after Queen Anne style, circa 1900. With H-stretchers. Set of eight . . . **$2,800**

English Victorian reproductions of generally Georgian chairs. Set of six, in mahogany . . . **$2,000**

English dining-room set, circa 1900. Chairs have Chippendale legs and high Jacobean-style backs, William and Mary cross stretchers. Table and chairs . . . **$2,500**

Queen Anne-style chairs made in England around 1900. Curved backs, squared corners of backs, and carving of back slats are all Victorian "improvements" on Queen Anne style. Set of eight . . . $3,300

Queen Anne or Georgian-style chairs made 1880–1900 in dark mahogany. Set of eight . . . $3,500

Rare ladder-back Chippendale chairs of English Victorian vintage. Set of eight . . . $2,800

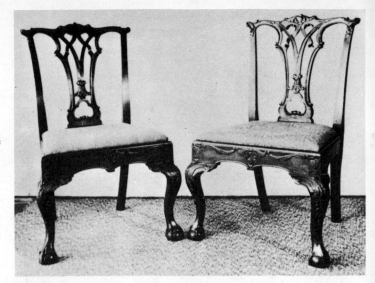

Exceptionally true Chippendale design with carving in the front rail. This set of eight English Victorian reproductions . . . **$4,000**

English Victorian reproduction Chippendale chairs with Gothic arches in backs. Set of eight . . . **$3,200**

Chinese Chippendale English Victorian reproductions straight from Chippendale's design book. Lacquered, pagoda tops. The pair . . .
   $1,800

Six examples of Chippendale dining sets made in England during *their* Victorian Era. Two armchairs and six straight chairs per set. Mahogany. They are commonly called "Centennial," as their "period" coincides with the American Centennial period of 1876 to about 1900.
$2,300–$2,800

Two single armchairs of English Victorian origin with style elements of Queen Anne and George I. For either one . . .
$450

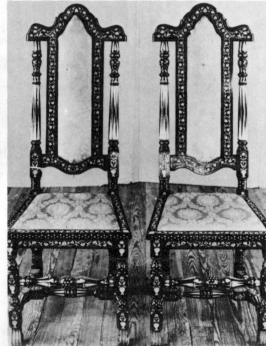

American Victorian chairs, circa 1880, Renaissance/Eastlake. For these two chairs . . .
$650

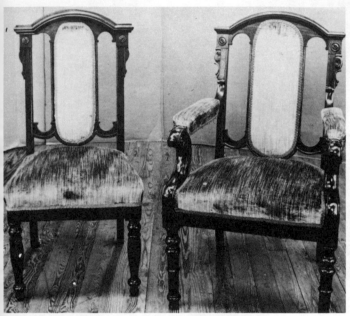

Jacobean-style chairs with a Moroccan influence, made in Victorian England on a dare. Ebonized wood with ivory inlay. The pair . . .
$1,500

In style, these two chairs are excellent examples of the transition between Queen Anne and Chippendale—i.e., Georgian or George II. Walnut, with balloon seats, strong splats. If they were authentic (1760), they would be worth twice as much as they are in this Victorian reproduction version. For the pair . . .
$1,250

English Victorian slipper chair in the Sheraton manner, solid mahogany.
$200

English Victorian chairs in the French and Italian manner, made of mahogany. Per chair . . .
$200

American Victorian chairs or love seats of French inspiration. The pair . . .
$600

An example of an unsuccessful Victorian attempt to combine Georgian styles, gross carving. Single chair . . .
$150

Queen Anne walnut library chair with duck feet, an example of a variation from style standards when the term "Georgian" is used. In this case, George I.
$1,500

More a Victorian "creation" than a reproduction of anything. A common chair in England.
$240

Queen Anne high-back dining chairs upholstered in leather. Custom-made. Each . . .
$400

Most popular of the late-Victorian English reproductions were fairly close copies of the Queen Anne style, such as these chairs. In sets of four . . .
$550

Excellent English Victorian reproduction of Chippendale chair. Single chair . . .
$500

Fine lacquered Chinese Chippendale armchair, a faithful Victorian reproduction.
$750

Authentic Chinese Chippendale armchair in mahogany, circa 1780.
$1,800

Oversized Chippendale reproduction, circa 1880, with superbly carved ribbon back—out of the design book.
$900

Ornate English armchair in the style of George II—a very Frenchified Queen Anne leading into the Chippendale codification of this idea. Made in U.S. circa 1900. Centennial.
$850

American chair of the late 1800s. Reproduction of classic Philadelphia Chippendale design—with eagle heads on the arms. An American Centennial chair.
$500

Unusually dumpy-looking "Chippendale" reproduction. Still, someone may pay . . .
$250

English Victorian chair combining many design characteristics. Very well built and known to have sold for as high as . . .
$500

Custom-made English reproduction chairs with tufted leather upholstery. Circa 1975. Per chair . . .
$600

Upholstered Sheraton shield-back chairs of the period in light mahogany. For the sophisticated buyer. The pair . . .
$1,600

Louis XV needlepoint chair reproduced in France about 1870–80. Walnut.
$500

Pair of French walnut cane-back chairs with cross stretchers. Regency out of Louis XV style. The pair . . .
$850

Gold-leafed Louis XV chair, cabriole legs with scroll feet. Circa 1890.
$500

Large, handsome Louis XV armchair in carved walnut. Circa 1890.
$750

98

Ebonized Louis XV chairs with gilded bronze mounts (ormolu), leather upholstery. Fairly recent reproductions. The pair . . . **$700**

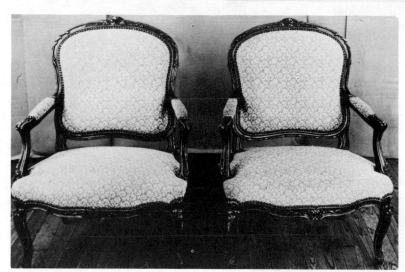

Good reproductions of Louis XV in walnut, late 1800s. The pair . . .
$1,000

99

Fauteuil (open-armed) French needlepoint chair in Louis XV style. Painted and gilded. Made about 1880. Each . . .
$450

Louis XVI-style carved walnut chair. Custom-made, U.S. reproduction.
$350

American version of a "French" chair made circa 1920. Bergère, gold highlighting on carving.
$400

Late Louis XV chairs with bergère (filled-in) arms, both very desirable and rare. Finely carved walnut. Reproduced in France in the late 1800s, still for the pair . . .
$1,300

Louis XVI-style chair in carved
walnut. Victorian Era
reproduction.
$600

Louis XVI chair with Aubusson
tapestry, carved walnut.
Reproduction, late 1800s.
$900

Painted Italian or Venetian chair,
circa 1890.
$450

American Victorian approach to
Louis XV with a remarkable shell
back of carved walnut, stained a
pale red. For the truly eclectic
collector.
$450

American Victorian mahogany
chair in the French manner.
$450

Carved teak palace chair imported
from China to England in
mid-1800s.
$600

American Victorian version of a
Queen Anne chair in oak.
$250

Pair of American Victorian
armchairs, circa 1860, finger
moulding, horsehair upholstery.
Pair . . .
$650

Rockers

Boston rocker with heavy pine
seat.
$155

Bow-back Windsor in the coarser
style of early 1800s, sold in kits to
be assembled by farmers. Springs
were a Shaker idea and make a
comfortable rocker.
$650

Victorian-made child's rocker—in
spite of the bamboo turnings that
look earlier.
$85

Bow-back rocker with added comb for shawl. Carpet cutter.
$850

Popular American Empire version of about 1830 with Boston-rocker arms, original decoration. A fiddleback Mammy Rocker with removable fence for baby.
$585

Hoop-skirt rocker in mostly tiger maple. Carpet-cutter rockers may be original or an early conversion in early 1800s. One of Ben Franklin's ideas.
$450

Small, but not child-size, carpet cutter. Obvious conversion of a simple stick-back Windsor side chair. Maple with pine seat.
$145

English broad-arm Windsor chair of oak, circa 1760, made into a rocker.
$450

Mammy Rocker with removable banister section in early southern style. Pine.
$435

Early American ladder-back rocker with nice patina and old finish.
$225

Child-size arrow-back rocker in pine and maple. Early 1800s. Apparently conversion from chair.
$135

Small rocker for adults from early 1800s. Maple and pine. New England.
$145

Upholstered

Period wing chair with good gold
damask upholstery. American
woods in Chippendale stretcher.
$2,200

Sheraton-style Massachusetts wing
chair in walnut with usable damask
fabric. Block-and-turn stretcher is
unusual. Reeded legs, brass casters.
$1,600

Beyond the Boston rocker. An
upholstered bergère rocker with a
loose seat. Made in Massachusetts
circa 1830.
$450

Custom-made Louis XV bergère
armchair (closed arms) with loose
seat. Walnut. Carving in Provincial
manner.
$375

Chippendale straight-back upholstered chair. Frame of the period, covered with appropriate new gold damask fabric.
$1,800

Queen Anne-style wing chair from New England circa 1750. Block-and-turn stretchers.
$2,700

Custom Louis XVI bergère chair, gilded and antique white.
$275

Authentic Chippendale wing chair rebuilt and reupholstered.
$2,100

108

Early-Victorian or Lincoln-period rocker. Reupholstered. Rose carving, solid mahogany.
$325

Shield-back early-Victorian armchair with good finger carving. Solid walnut, rebuilt and refinished.
$400

Original frame Chippendale wing chair, rebuilt and reupholstered.
$2,500

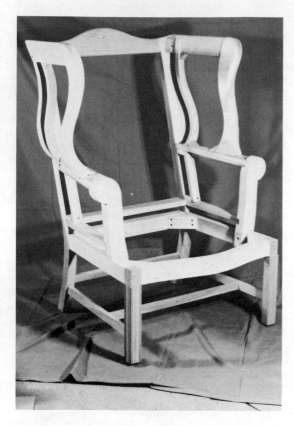

Custom-built reproduction frame of a Chippendale shaped-wing armchair with stretcher base. As upholstered chair, depending on quality of fabric . . .
$500–$800

Reproduction Hepplewhite frame with stretcher base. As upholstered chair, depending on quality of fabric . . .
$400–$700

Custom-made in England, a Chippendale-style wing chair upholstered in (ugh!) black leather.
$650

110

French wing chair in the style of
the late 1600s, roughly Louis XIV,
made in early 1900s.
$650

American-made 1920 version of a
Queen Anne wing chair.
Apiece . . .
$450

Reupholstered Queen Anne wing
chair of the period, with
claw-and-ball foot made
mid-to-late 1700s.
$1,500

111   An American Victorian chair made
about 1890 out of Louis XV with
paw feet. Gilded walnut, and a
certain lack of restraint in
decoration. For the eclectic
collector.
$1,100

Authentic Queen Anne wing
chair made in England, circa 1770,
mahogany.
$1,700

Chippendale mahogany wing chair
with square Marlborough legs and
scroll arm. Of the period : . .
$1,500

A French chair in the transitional
style between Louis XIV and Louis
XV, circa 1710–15. As it is a
reproduction made in the late
1800s . . .
$750

112

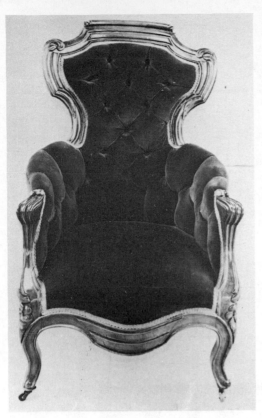

American Victorian mahogany (circa 1860) French-manner wing chair. Reupholstered.
$475

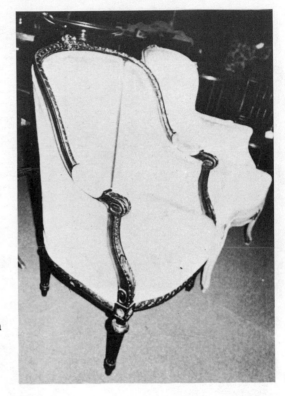

Barrel-back Louis XVI bergère chair. Made in America, custom reproduction.
$400

Pair of Louis XVI bergère (closed arm) chairs, gold-leafed over gesso with pumice dust in crevices. Reupholstered. Circa 1890.
$1,250

CHESTS

Lift-top

Country-made pine workchest with
original paint, early 1800s.
$225

Pine settle or storage bench, circa
1830, New England.
$450

Unusual curved bracket feet on
walnut lift-top blanket chest with
dovetailed corners. American.
Hard to date, but 1700s.
$625

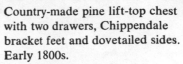

Country-made pine lift-top chest with two drawers, Chippendale bracket feet and dovetailed sides. Early 1800s.
$350

Lift-top blanket chest with artificial graining, painted inlay strips, Hepplewhite French feet. In fact, imitation Hepplewhite. American, circa 1830. All on pine.
$525

Typical New England blanket chest from mid-1700s with one drawer and lift top. Has original old paint on wide boards. Strap hinges, built-in ditty box.
$450

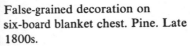

False-grained decoration on six-board blanket chest. Pine. Late 1800s.
$225

Top of early blanket chest that has been cut off and mounted on coasters as coffee table. False front drawers. Window seat, storage. Original red paint.

$275

Typical six-board pine blanket chest, circa 1800, with bootjack feet (extensions of solid ends). Refinished.

$280

Early sea chest (late 1700s) with original paint, woven rope handles at ends. Ubiquitous in New England because there were mostly one-trip sailors in whaling days.

$150

Six-board pine blanket chest with secret compartment under built-in ditty box or till. Mid-1800s. Refinished . . .

$250

Late sea chest (mid-1800s) with wrought-iron handles. As is . . . $75

Bun feet show influence of Empire style on this six-board blanket chest/sea chest/window seat. As is . . . $200

Overrefinished dough box with cover from province of Quebec. $140

Excellent early sea chest with slant front, original woven rope handles in side beckets, hand-wrought strap hinges, original pale-blue finish on wide pine boards. $350

New England pine blanket chest
with fine dovetailing and two
drawers, bracket feet, inlay on
drawers, circa 1760.
   $1,200

English blanket chest with carved
initials, circa 1690, made of
walnut Pre-Queen Anne period
Renaissance feeling.
   $750

Antique Korean chest of elm, circa
1840. Front opens out.
   $575

English oak country blanket chest,
circa 1760, bracket feet.
   $700

American piece with splayed
French-style feet. Cherry. Circa
1800.
    $1,200

Pine chest of six drawers in
original grain-painted decoration.
Original knobs. Circa 1840.
Pennsylvania/Virginia origin.
    $425

119

Miniature mahogany chest with
ogee bracket feet, and lift-top pine
blanket chest with three false
drawers on top, circa 1740.
American.
    $250 and **$750**

New England bachelor's chest under Chippendale influence, with Hepplewhite lightness seen in bracket feet and brasses.
$850

American highboy base that was converted into lowboy by addition of new top when upper case was removed—probably for use as chest of drawers in a bedroom. Queen Anne legs and Chippendale skirt date it circa 1750.
$1,400

American lowboy with trifid feet on bottom of Queen Anne legs. Made of walnut in early 1700s.
$2,500

American four-drawer Chippendale chest in tiger maple with fine ogee feet. Original Hepplewhite brasses.
$1,800

Country-made, circa 1760, somewhere in England. "Hepplewhite" standard chest of drawers in oak.
$750

American walnut chest with graduated drawers, circa 1760. Replacement Hepplewhite brasses.
$1,200

121

American Hepplewhite serpentine-front chest with inlaid shell in the skirt. Mahogany, circa 1800.
$1,400

Portuguese bombé chest of
drawers. Mahogany, circa 1780.
$2,500

British military campaign chest in
streaked paducah wood (like
mahogany). Separates into two
sections for easier carrying by
handles on ends. Flush drawer
pulls for stacking. Late 1700s.
$1,100

Philadelphia chest of drawers with
reeded corner columns, applied
moulding around rim of top. Top
overhangs at back. Dust dividers.
Bulky bracket feet.
$4,800

122

Serpentine-front transitional piece between Hepplewhite and Chippendale. Circa 1780. New England. Cherry.
$8,500

Twentieth-century copy of Rhode Island design block-front chest in mahogany.
$1,700

Massachusetts oxbow chest, circa 1750. Shaped top, bulky feet, original bail pulls. Figured mahogany.
$12,000

Jacobean oak chest made circa
1690.
$1,100

Jacobean-style oak chest with
drawer mouldings and pulls of the
period. Mounted on Chippendale
bracket feet—inappropriately.
$475

Early Jacobean chest made of oak,
circa 1690.
$1,200

William and Mary chest on stand,
circa 1710. Walnut. Strong bun
feet.
$1,550

William and Mary Jacobean-style chest with moulding on drawer fronts, turnip feet, pendant pulls, paneled ends. Oak, circa 1710.
$1,700

Queen Anne-style burl-walnut chest of drawers, with considerable restoration and replacement parts faked in.
$1,300

Custom-made faithful reproduction of Queen Anne walnut lowboy, made in England circa 1925.
$450

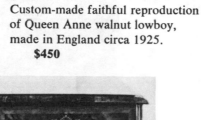

Queen Anne bachelor's chest of burl walnut with replacement bracket feet. Made about 1740.
$1,500

Queen Anne-style chest with bracket feet.
$600

Oyster-walnut Queen Anne chest of drawers, circa 1730. Original bun feet replaced by bracket feet—such replacements being necessary with the majority of such chests of the period. Even so . . .
$2,000

Hepplewhite chest of drawers, circa 1800, with divided upper drawers, which indicates English origin. Mahogany with pencil-line inlay.
$1,200

Sheraton chest of drawers with turreted legs and D-front, from Massachusetts or New York, circa 1810. Mahogany veneers.
$1,500

Pure Hepplewhite chest of highest quality made in U.S. Secret top center drawer, original brasses, flame mahogany.
$3,200

Bow-front chest according to
Hepplewhite, with Chippendale
ogee bracket feet, in mahogany.
$2,200

Bow-front Georgian chest of
drawers, circa 1780. Spade feet,
flame-mahogany veneer, strange
replacement brasses.
$750

English chest in mahogany with
clumsy replacement feet. But top is
of the period—George III.
$750

Excellent English fake (i.e.,
distressed reproduction) with inlaid
burl-walnut drawer fronts in the
"Early Georgian" style.
$1,200

127

Hepplewhite/George III chest of drawers with nice skirt and splayed feet, circa 1790.
$750

English mahogany bachelor's chest with a writing slide, circa 1760. Chippendale with Hepplewhite-style inlay strips on drawers.
$1,200

English Hepplewhite bachelor's chest, circa 1780, splayed feet. Mahogany.
$750

Small Hepplewhite chest in mahogany, circa 1780.
$800

English secretary-chest, circa 1890, in Hepplewhite manner except for Sheraton legs. Top drawer front falls down for writing surface, drawers and cubbyholes inside.
$1,000

Hepplewhite bachelor's chest in flame mahogany.
$850

Hepplewhite drawered chest with Chippendale bracket feet and Empire wooden knobs. Circa 1880.
$750

English secretary-chest, circa 1890, with Hepplewhite inlays in mahogany, Louis XVI legs. Sometimes called butler's chests.
$1,200

British military campaign chest, circa 1760, in flamè-grain mahogany. Built-in secretary behind one drawer front.
$1,200

English bachelor's chest in Georgian/Chippendale style, circa 1920, with burl-walnut veneer drawer fronts.
$600

130

Small bachelor's chests for use as
end tables with writing slides.
Made of solid and veneered
walnut. Modern reproductions that
are prime candidates for instant
aging Each . . .
  $350

French Provincial walnut
three-drawer chest, also loosely
called a commode. Block front.
Circa 1770 or earlier.
  $2,700

French Provincial chest of the
period with unusual—but
authentic—block front. Figured
walnut or unidentifiable fruitwood.
  $2,800

French Provincial small chest or
commode in fruitwood. Ormolu
mounts.
  $1,800

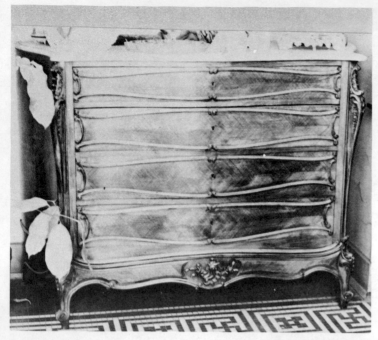

Light walnut marquetry bedroom chest in the manner of Louis XV, circa 1910.
$650

A rare authentic French Provincial chest in walnut, circa 1750, with rococo bronze handles which are correct and original.
$2,500

Victorian reproduction of a Louis XVI chest with ivory inlays. Mahogany.
$450

132

American Empire chest, circa
1820, in solid and veneer
mahogany. Spiral posts with
pineapple tops.
$850

American Empire chest by Rufus
Piece of Boston, circa 1830. Solid
and veneer mahogany.
$1,800

Louis XVI French Provincial
walnut chest that has been
lacquered and given a marble top.
The gilded lily . . .
$750

A miniature of a larger piece of furniture, this jewelry box is about 20 inches tall. American Empire, circa 1850, crotch mahogany veneers. Rare in Empire.
$300

American Empire bureau with dressing mirror in crotch mahogany veneer, white marble top. Halfway into pillar-and-scroll or bandsaw style, (late) American Empire.
$550

134

Very early American Victorian on Renaissance style. Walnut, glued-on carving, white marble top.
$650

Tall

An unusual pair of semainiers, as both have an extra eighth drawer. Veneered with marquetry. Gilded bronze ormolu mounts. Of the Louis XVI/Directoire period. Made circa 1900. For the pair . . .
    $1,800

Victorian American walnut chest of drawers with bonnet cabinet. Burl walnut. Circa 1900. Indefinite Renaissance style.
    $575

Semainier of the Second Empire, white marble top, brass inlay and bronze ormolu mounts on ebonized wood. An ugly duckling, but of the period.
    $800

Serpentine-front bedroom chest
painted in manner of Angelica
Kauffmann. Custom-made in U.S.
circa 1920.
$1,500

Louis XV seven-drawer semainiers.
Marquetry veneered in kingwood,
rosewood, and satinwood. Made in
U.S. circa 1920. The pair . . .
$1,500

American Empire chest, circa
1840. Figured mahogany on pine.
Unusual original brasses.
$800

American high chest with graduated drawers, circa 1730. Scraped maple, with remnants of original red milk paint.
$3,400

French tall bedroom chest with white marble top, marquetry drawer fronts, simple cabriole legs. Such marquetry pieces are a subdivision of the Louis XV style and were usually mounted with ormolu, but this is an exceptionally restrained example. Of the period . . .
$2,500

An authentic country English oak chest in the William and Mary style. Called a highboy or high chest. Made in early 1700s.
$1,600

English oak chest, circa 1760, of
the period.
$750

Pine bonnet chest, circa 1850, with
original wooden knobs.
$750

Early American piece appealing to
the serious collector even though
the bracket feet and the cross
board are missing. Six graduated
drawers, Chippendale inspiration,
mid-1700s. In present
condition . . .
$1,600

Bonnet chest (two square
drawers), circa 1850s. Made of
chestnut, pine, cherry, and
butternut. Style elements of
Empire (case), Chippendale
(bracket feet), and Hepplewhite
(drawer edging and reproduction
brasses that replace original flat,
round knobs).
$850

138

Five-drawer New England Chippendale chest with bracket feet. Reproduction brasses, plain maple.
$1,800

American Empire chest with three drawers on top and rope-carved post is early version, circa 1810–20. Crotch-grain mahogany veneer on pine and mahogany base wood.
$450

Typical American Chippendale-style six-drawer chest with New England simplicity. Maple. 1750–80.
$2,400

Early American six-drawer chest in birch, graduated drawers, important top moulding, feet reflecting Queen Anne period in England, circa 1700. Not for sale in present condition. Fully restored . . .
$2,300

Queen Anne maple chest on frame from Connecticut, circa 1750. All parts original, including frame with cabriole legs with pad feet.
$6,500

New England Hepplewhite-style tall chest made of maple with a mahogany stain. Inappropriate brasses. Circa 1778.
$2,700

Chest-on-Chest

English chest-on-chest, circa 1800,
moving into Regency style, in
flame-grain mahogany.
$2,400

English chest-on-chest in flame
mahogany, writing slide. Circa
1800.
$2,200

English chest-on-chest with writing
slide in well-figured mahogany,
circa 1760. Superior cabinet work.
$2,600

Smallish English chest-on-chest
made circa 1790, writing slide, but
inferior wood and dark finish.
$1,900

English chest-on-chest made in late
1700s of mahogany. French pulls.
$2,400

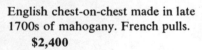

English chest-on-chest made in late
1700s of elm. With writing slide.
$2,100

Hepplewhite chest-on-chest with Italian (?) pediments.
$2,200

English mahogany chest-on-chest with bracket feet and fretwork on top. Late 1700s.
$2,200

Richly inlaid William and Mary chest-on-stand, barley-twist legs. English Victorian reproduction.
$2,500

Victorian copy of a chest-on-chest in style transitional from William and Mary (legs and stretcher) to Queen Anne. Figured walnut.
$3,300

English chest-on-chest in three parts (pediment is separate). Adam/Hepplewhite with French feet. Flame-grain mahogany. Bow front. Top has cross-banded frieze, four plinths and an inlaid conch shell. Circa 1780, all original.
$3,800

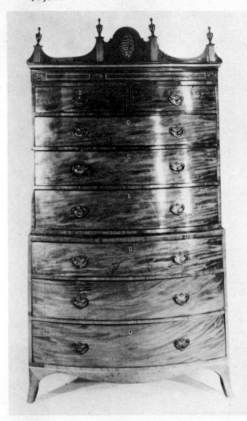

American chest-on-chest of maple, all original except brasses. Circa 1760.
$4,500

Cherry chest-on-chest with good
proportions. Connecticut style.
$12,000

Chest-on-chest in cherry.
Country-made, shell carving on
top. Circa 1790. American origin.
$3,800

Chest-on-chest in cherry with short
Chippendale bracket feet. Made in
England in the late 1800s.
$2,200

CHINA CABINETS

Late-Victorian or "Golden oak"
round china cabinet made in U.S.
circa 1900. Good carving.
   $700

French Victorian walnut display
cabinet with extra-fine carving.
Circa 1880.
   $1,800

Carved Chinese china cabinet,
circa 1880, for export to England.
   $850

146

French Art Modern parlor case
made in London, circa 1900.
$900

Louis XV china cabinet with vernis
martin panels, gilded frame, made
about 1880.
$1,500

Chinese Chippendale-style china
cabinet made in England, circa
1900. Mahogany, blind fretwork.
$1,250

147

Large French vitrine in Louis XVI
style in spite of the feet, made
around 1880–90. Strong cabinet
work. Antique white.
$2,300

Louis XVI round vitrine, with
brass inlay and ormolu mounts,
made around 1900.
$1,800

Louis XVI
all-wood vitrine,
square,
carved, and gilded.
Circa 1890.
$1,300

148

Mahogany Louis XVI vitrine or
china cabinet with gilded bronze
mounts. Lots of glass. Made 1890.
$1,600

Louis XV china case, antique gold.
Flower paintings, ormolu mounts.
$900

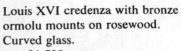

Louis XVI credenza with bronze
ormolu mounts on rosewood.
Curved glass.
$1,500

Carved walnut, very rococo Louis
XV-design display cabinet.
$1,575

Very good Louis XV-style vitrine.
Marquetry covered bombé front of
kingwood, tulipwood, satinwood,
ormolu mounts. Made 1860.
$2,500

Serpentine-front vitrine in antique
gold paint with vernis martin
panels. Louis XV-style, circa 1900.
   $1,450

Louis XV china cabinet in antique
gold paint and vernis martin decorative
panels. Circa 1180.
   $1,250

French Victorian, or Second
Empire, stained walnut display
cabinet, circa 1860.
   $850

150

Boulle inlaid credenza, ebonized,
heavy ormolu mounts, white
marble top. Style of Second
Empire. Made 1860.
$1,500

Louis XV vitrine made circa 1870,
ebonized, scenic panel, etc.
$1,500

Louis XVI-style gilt vitrine, made
about 1870.
$1,350

Concave glass-front vitrine,
mahogany, ormolu, brass gallery
on top.
      $1,450

Bonheur du jour in Louis XV
marquetry kingwood, ormolu
mounts. Made 1870.
      $1,500

CLOCKS

Connecticut-made pillar-and-scroll clock, circa 1820. Fine apron, makers paper inside.
$1,500

Empire ogee clock, circa 1830. Maple and mahogany veneer. Brass works and label inside.
$225

Victorian walnut mantel clock. Label inside, eight-day brass movement, striking all the way.
$145

Victorian oak mantel clock, eight-day brass movement, striking on hour and half-hour. Called "gingerbread" clock.
$125

Beehive mantel clock with rosewood case and reverse painting, circa 1840.
$265

Seth Thomas-labeled clock from Connecticut, circa 1830–40. Mahogany veneer and gilded columns, eight-day brass movement.
$650

Tall English case clock, circa 1850. Figured mahogany veneer, eight-day movement, signed.
$950

Standing clock with brass dial built in 1770 by John Avary in Connecticut. Cherry case (also Connecticut) has ogee feet pineapple finials, fan on door.
$8,500

154

Victorian Renaissance-style clock with brass works. Walnut case.
$175

Simple country-built grandfather clock case with factory-made one-day brass movement. Overrefinished, but with fine hand-painted face on wood, signed V. E. Edwards, Ashby, 1790.
$1,400

Face of preceding clock by V. E. Edwards.

Ubiquitous mid-Victorian beehive mantel clock in rosewood and walnut case.
$175

American Empire mantel clock
with veneered ogee top and base.
Rosewood on pine. Reverse
painting on glass.
$145

Regulator-type mid-Victorian (and
later) wall clock used in offices for
workers to set their watches by.
Many fakes from Japan. This
authentic one . . .
$200

French clock in a dome made
around 1850 on bronze base.
$850

George Washington clock made in
France for American Centennial
celebration, circa 1876.
$700

White marble and ormolu clock
with Wedgewood plaque, made
circa 1870.
$1,200

Light-blue Sèvres clock, made in
France in 1860.
$850

French Empire clock. Rosewood
case inlaid with satinwood.
$850

French garniture clock and
candlestands, white marble,
ormolu.
$1,500

Pillar-and-scroll clock made in
U.S. in 1750.
$1,500

French bisque clock made in
mid-1800s.
$850

158

Classical French Empire clock
garniture with two urns, white
marble, made 1810—of the period.
$1,400

Gilded bronze and white marble
Louis XV-style mantel clock, made
about 1870.
$1,100

French Victorian copy of a Louis
XVI clock, white marble,
garniture.
$1,250

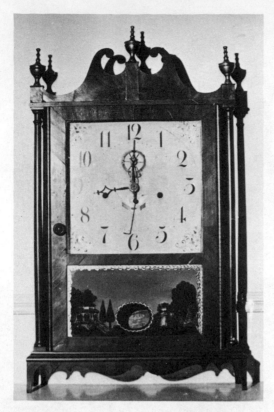

Eli Terry pillar-and-scroll clock with release mechanism in front of face.
$3,100

Late 1800s French mantel clocks made of gilded white metal. Rococo Louis XV design.
Each . . .
$600

Art deco marble clock with bronze figures and two other bronze figures mounted on marble.
Each . . .
$500

Typical English mantel clock in black marble mount. Circa 1900.
$300

White marble Empire clock with ormolu mounts.
$800

Rouge marble, bronze garniture clock and two urns, circa 1900.
$825

Three-piece French clock set to grace a mantel. Bronze and marble, made in Victorian Era. **$2,000**

English Victorian calendar clock. Walnut case, bronze dial, and falling numbers. Used in hotels. **$650**

English Victorian clock with eight bells in oak case. A master timer. **$1,250**

Tall

Chippendale-style cherry case
made in U.S. about 1810. Brass
dial and English works, circa 1750,
signed by the maker.
$2,500

American cherry case, circa 1800,
which has been adapted to hold
clock with smaller dial of painted
wood. Eagle finial.
$1,200

Maple case with brass dial made in
Maine, circa 1790, by Paul Rogers.
$5,500

English clock, circa 1820, with
round face of the period.
$1,600

Oak and mahogany English case
with rising moon dial, circa 1800.
$1,600

New England clock with
Roxbury-type scroll, circa 1810.
Cherry case.
$3,200

Cherry-case tall clock with
Roxbury-type scroll fretwork,
ebonized trim detail. Enamel dial.
New England, circa 1800.
$3,500

Country-made New England clock,
circa 1820, with wooden works,
30-hour movement, run by
weights. Wind-up holes on dial are
painted on.
$1,600

164

New England tall clock with
cherry case, enameled dial.
Unsigned.
$3,300

French tall-case clock of provincial origin, circa 1800. Large brass pendulum with lyre. Walnut case.
$1,800

Lacquered chinoiserie clock made in England in 1780 in the style of George III. Brass face and chimes.
$2,300

Light oak English tall-case clock made 1780. Painted wood face with mahogany top, shell inlay.
$1,250

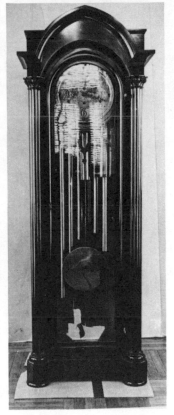

English tall-case clock from 1890 with excellent movement and Westminster-type chimes, brass face, and moving moon.
$2,600

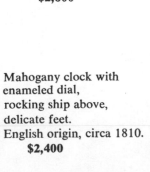

Mahogany clock with enameled dial, rocking ship above, delicate feet. English origin, circa 1810.
$2,400

U.S.-made Victorian case clock, circa 1900, in Empire style with eight-strike tube chimes, brass face.
$2,000

Wall

Continental wall-bracket clock.
$350

French three-weight country wall
clock of brass with enamel face.
$900

Reproduction of a wag-on-the-wall
clock made in France. Metal
pendulum is very thin—almost a
foil.

$125

COMMODES

Louis XV commode with gray-and-white marble top, ormolu mounted. King, tulip, and other woods.
$2,000

Rococo French commode made circa 1870 in kingwood and heavily ormolu (gilded bronze) mounted, rouge marble top, bombé front.
$2,500

Italian painted bombé commode with Louis XVI legs, gilded.
$600

French bronze-mounted commode or hall sideboard. Circa 1880, marble top in the manner of Louis XVI moving into Empire.
$2,000

Spanish-made, circa 1920, reproduction of Louis XV commode with Sèvres plaques, king, tulip and other woods, inlaid flowers, ormolu mounts.
$1,600

French credenza in Louis XV style with marble top, fine inlay work.
$1,400

Pair of boulle Second Empire side cabinets made in France about 1875. White marble tops. Each . . .
$850

French Victorian washstand of
rosewood with white marble top.
$550

Very long French Provincial
credenza in walnut. Authentic.
$2,200

Mid-1800s reproduction of
demilune satinwood commode,
painted in the manner of Angelica
Kauffmann. Adam style.
$2,400

French Victorian credenza made of rosewood with marble top.
$850

Louis XV drop-front desk in marquetry of king, satin, and tulip woods.
$1,400

Biedermeier piece, the German version of French Empire. Authentic, circa 1815. Burl walnut. Rare.
$1,400

170

French Provincial walnut commode with drawer in fine condition.
$1,550

English painted commode of pine with marble top, circa 1840.
$575

Louis XV revival bedroom piece. Walnut, rococo carving, 1890.
$1,250

Pair of Adam-style satinwood side cabinets used as pedestals. Custom-made in U.S. Each . . . **$450**

French bedside commodes, marble lined. Walnut, made 1850. Each . . . **$225**

CUPBOARDS AND DRESSERS

Early standing wall cupboard with very wide boards, beading.
$450

Hanging wall cupboard with false reddish graining. Early or mid-1800s. Pine.
$275

Pine wall cupboard from early 1800s with Chippendale bracket feet, good moulding on top and beading.
$1,100

New England dresser or flat cupboard, circa 1785, with raised panels and strong beading. Pine.
$900

Pine dresser with bottom from early 1800s, to which a supposedly Colonial-style top has been tastelessly added.
$850

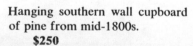
Hanging southern wall cupboard of pine from mid-1800s.
$250

Centennial pine hutch cupboard made in late 1800s. Fine cabinet work with beading around doors, drawers, and shelves.
$850

Country-made American cupboard in painted pine. Mid-1800s.
$585

Mid-1800s mahogany cupboard bookcase, made in England along Empire lines.
$650

Connecticut blind-door cherry cupboard with raised panels in doors. Circa 1780s.
$1,600

English burl-walnut linen press, circa 1715. Concave shell on bottom inside sunburst inlay. Fine Queen Anne.
$7,200

Flat cupboard with top door removed and aperture reshaped. Raised panel door, circa 1800, but supposed to look older.
$900

New England dresser from the late 1700s, used for displaying family pewter. Pine.
$1,600

English hanging corner cupboard with drawers below. Walnut.
$350

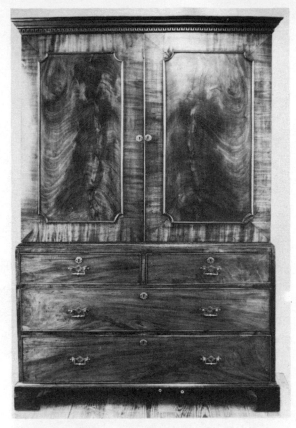

English linen press, circa 1780 style, with spectacular veneering. Shelves inside cupboard slide out.
$2,100

Hepplewhite linen press made in mid-1800s in rosewood with fret-cut swan-neck broken arch, Chippendale feet, Adam inlay. Typical Victorian treatment of eighteenth-century styles.
$1,600

Queen Anne fitted cabinet, circa 1730, but feet replaced with French-influence ones. Unusual authentic hinges on mirror-fronted doors. Burl walnut.
$7,600

177

Welsh dresser in usual oak, circa
early 1700s. Original pendant
pulls, back replacement.
$3,200

French provincial cupboard of
fine-figured walnut, circa 1750.
$2,300

Welsh country-made dresser. Oak
with wooden pulls.
$2,400

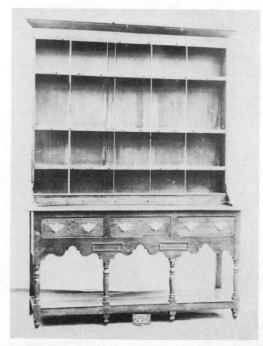

Welsh dresser made of oak,
country piece, circa 1760.
$2,300

French Provincial cupboard with glass doors in walnut. Made about 1760.
$2,400

American factory-made white reproduction of an English breakfront, circa 1945. "Early Bronx."
$795

Cabinet on stand made in U.S., circa 1920. Black lacquered, inlaid. Base combines styles of William and Mary (stretcher) and Queen Anne/Chippendale legs with Louis XV scroll feet. Chinese Chippendale top. Life is a cabaret!
$995.50

Antique white finish on a
reproduction cupboard with
vaguely French lines. Circa 1930.
$795

Heavily carved Victorian cupboard
made in India, circa 1880, of a nice
oriental wood. Brass moulding
around glass.
$1,500

Something made up of old wood
and of no particular merit, possibly
French.
$299.50

180

Corner Cupboards

Early American corner cupboard, circa 1790, with shaped porringer shelves and Queen Anne-style curves on face mouldings. Raised panel door. All authentic.
$1,600

Corner cabinet made of rosewood, circa 1850, in Germany. Cross between imitation Louis XV and Biedermeier.
$1,250

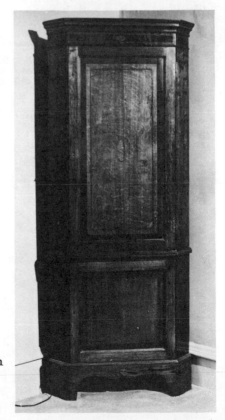

English oak corner cupboard with inlay at top. Country-made in mid-1700s.
$1,450

Cherry corner cupboard from New England, circa 1800, with raised panels and bold English cut-out on skirt, Empire cornice.
$1,250

Corner cabinet made of oak, circa 1780. English.
$1,100

Hard pine cupboard, country-made in early 1800s with fine fat Chippendale ogee bracket feet. Virginia origin.
$2,600

182

Cherry corner cupboard, circa 1820. Wood indicates Pennsylvania or New Jersey origin.
$1,100

Pine corner cupboard made in two parts. Raised panels, beading, unusual raised moulding, original bracket feet. American, circa 1760.
$3,600

183

Walnut corner cupboard from Virginia, early 1800s. Most glass panes original.
$1,250

Two-part mahogany corner cupboard. Glassed arched door with fifteen panels of original glass. Early 1800s. Old finish.
$1,450

Painted corner cupboard. Yellow, nice patina, western Massachusetts, pine. Mid-1700s.
$1,800

Walnut corner cupboard of southern (U.S.) origin. Pine, circa 1810. Old glass.
$1,200

Corner cupboard in solid walnut with original hardware and old glass, refinished. Of American Empire-into-Gothic period of mid-1800s.
$3,200

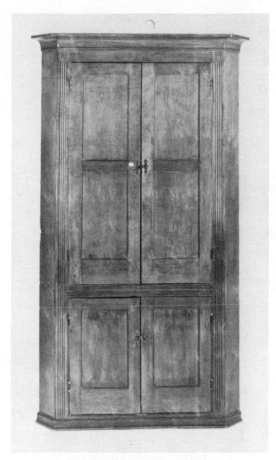

Cherry corner cupboard with reeded corner risers, old hardware, southern origin.
$2,700

185

Pine corner cupboard of mid-1800s. Painted and decorated later, but good lines.
$750

DAVENPORTS

Cylinder-top davenport made in China for British market, circa 1850. Papier-mâché, lacquered black with ivory and mother-of-pearl inlays.
$2,500

American Victorian walnut davenport or writing desk.
$850

Edwardian davenport with Chinese Chippendale blind fretwork, circa 1900. Mahogany with leather top.
$1,100

DECOYS

Although fine decoys are a collector's specialty, many simple but decorative ones, such as these, are available in the price range of . . .

$35-$150

Shore birds of special interest to collectors have been sold for as high as $10,000. However, many less than 100 years old, depending on the style, sell for . . .

$40-$300

DESKS

Baltimore-made Sheraton-style desk with figured mahogany doors, circa 1810. Top flips out to rest on supports.
$2,300

Victorian partner's desk of oak in the style of Early Vulgar.
$850

Boston-made tambour desk, circa 1800. Curled mahogany drawer facings after Hepplewhite, legs moving into Sheraton.
$12,000

Military chest with built-in desk. Camphorwood. Found in Bermuda. Brass pulls and handles on ends were made flush for close stacking on shipboard. Early example from early 1700s.
$1,600

American Hepplewhite desk with inlay of George Washington, tambour doors over flip-out desk. A Centennial piece, circa 1876, of course.
$3,200

Old-fashioned screw-down school desk and chair from early 1900s. American.
$75

Sheraton desk with flip-out top that rests on brackets. Figured mahogany veneers and inlaid drawers. Circa 1815.
$2,200

Butler's desk with Hepplewhite lines and brasses, typical French feet. Made in America of maple, birch, or cherry stained dark-red mahogany.
$1,800

Same desk opened.

Variation of Wells Fargo desk in walnut with leather slant front newly added. Refinished.
$800

Same desk with false pediment opened to show cubbyholes.

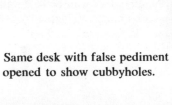

190

Wells Fargo desk of
early-Victorian Era but basically
American Empire-design features
such as pediment, legs, paneled
doors, but Victorian pulls.
Restored original finish. Walnut.
   $950

Same desk opened to show spaces
for ledgers and twelve cubbyholes
for monthly bills at top.

Cylinder Hepplewhite or
late-Georgian desk in mahogany
and satinwood, leather writing
surface.
   $1,850

English-made desk in Empire style
in walnut. Writing surface pulls
out, front comes off. Unusual.
   $1,600

191

Dutch cylinder desk, made 1859.
Mahogany with fancy marquetry.
$3,200

Unusual English piece, circa 1780.
A gentleman's dressing table in
flame mahogany with tambour top.
$850

Cylinder-top late-Georgian/
Hepplewhite, sliding writing
surface, circa 1790. Flame
mahogany, splayed feet.
$1,750

192

Hepplewhite drop-front butler's desk or secretary with shell inlay, French legs. Continental origin.
$1,350

French Empire cylinder desk, circa 1810. Mahogany and burl walnut, white marble top. Of the period . . .
$1,800

Continental roll-top desk made of satinwood with brass rails. Mid-1800s.
$1,550

Kneehole

Kidney-shaped desk of
Continental origin with marquetry
veneers, circa 1900.
$1,400

Three-part Chinese kneehole desk
in teak, circa 1870s.
$1,200

English kneehole desk with bracket
feet after Chippendale, circa 1890.
$350

Drop-front desk made in England, circa 1870. Oak.
$650

Kneehole desk after French Empire style, made in U.S., circa 1920.
$285

Georgian writing desk, circa 1780. Three-part, mahogany. Of the period.
$4,200

Eighteenth-century kneehole desk, Chippendale, mahogany, authentic.
$1,400

Flat-top desk of English origin but no great style. Mahogany veneer, leather top.
$850

English partner's desk, circa 1800, with mahogany veneers on walnut, original brass pulls. Lower three drawers on both sides are false fronts on cupboard doors.
$3,500

English three-part desk on ball-and-claw feet, circa 1900. Called partner's desk.
$1,800

American Victorian partner's desk,
circa 1870. Walnut.
$1,500

Three-part English desk of William
and Mary into Queen Anne style,
circa 1890. Burl walnut, curved
front.
$2,500

Extra-large Victorian partner's
desk of walnut, leather top.
$2,000

Roll-top

S-shaped roll top is most valuable style of oak office desks of early 1900s. Beautifully refinished.
$900

American Victorian s-curve, roll-top desk in oak with Wooten-type turn-out bottom cabinets. Circa 1880.
$1,800

English Victorian cylinder desk in
mahogany, with slide-out surface,
satinwood drawers. Made 1860.
      $1,250

English roll-top desk in oak.
Many drawers, pristine condition.
      $2,200

English Victorian cylinder desk,
mahogany and satinwood, with
slide-out surface. Wooden knobs,
wide.
      $1,350

Simple English Victorian oak roll top, s-curve.
$1,200

English s-curve in oak with roll top.
$1,200

Secret Drawer

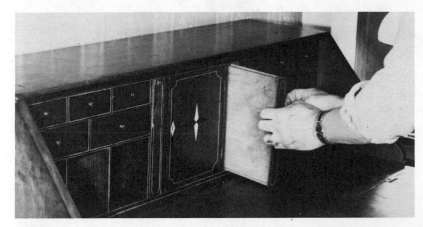

Secret drawers are frequently found in American slant-front desks of the 1700s. First photo shows removal by fingernail of concealed document drawer, one of the commonest hideaways.

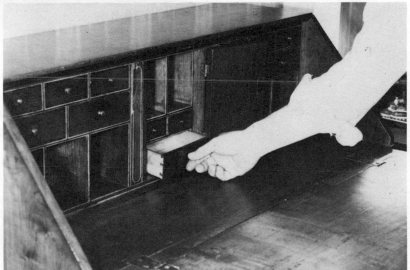

Center bottom drawer is removed . . .

so latch hidden under it can be depressed by fingertip . . .

releasing central box structure, which when slid out . . .

reveals drawer in back of it.

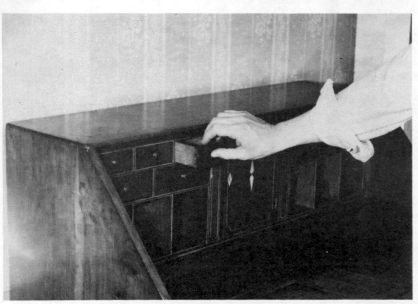

Also, by removing these two small drawers . . .

202

the divider between them can then be pulled out . . .

revealing secret boxes behind them.

203

Slant-front

American maple desk with unusual mould at bottom and bracket feet. Early 1800s, simple country piece.
$2,500

American-made Hepplewhite desk with French feet, simple interior, cherry.
$2,100

Rhode Island block-front mahogany desk with strong feet, Centennial, faithful copy.
$3,600

Slant-front desk (called *bureau* in England) in light mahogany. Hepplewhite with Chippendale bracket feet. Made in England, circa 1780.
$1,500

English slant-front desk in flame mahogany. Hepplewhite with bracket feet, circa 1780.
$1,400

Hepplewhite slant-front desk inlays and secret drawer in mahogany. Baltimore-design oval inlay front.
$2,600

Burl-walnut English slant-front desk, circa 1760. Queen Anne feeling.
$3,200

Chippendale slant-front desk in flame mahogany with ogee feet, made 1780.
$1,800

Unusually small (and more desirable) Georgian/Hepplewhite desk, circa 1870.
$2,200

Unusually small Georgian/Hepplewhite in less interesting wood than preceding desk.
$1,900

American cherry desk made in New England, circa 1770, with typical simplicity.
$2,500

Victorian English (1800s) version of Georgian slant front—vertical veneer on door fronts.
$1,200

French Provincial *bureau de dame*, circa 1760. Solid walnut with tulipwood and satinwood inlays.
$1,800

Centennial block-front mahogany desk in the classic Chippendale style—from the book.
$2,200

American Chippendale-style slant-front desk in curly maple, circa 1760–80. Ogee feet. Often called Governor Winthrop desk.
$4,000

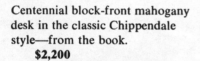

208

Queen Anne "schoolmaster's" desk from the Centennial or late-Victorian period in U.S.
$460

Slant-front Chippendale, or Governor Winthrop, desk made of wavy birch. From New England, circa mid-1700s.

$2,800

Same desk with front opened.

Maple Chippendale slant-top desk made in New England in 1770s. Original bracket feet, some hand carving, suitable replacement brasses.

$2,800

209

American applewood slant-front desk in the Hepplewhite style, with secret drawers. Because of definite American origin . . .
$2,500

Same desk opened.

An imported English Hepplewhite slant-front desk, selling for approximately half the price of preceding desk of American origin . . .
$1,300

William and Mary-style trumpet-legged, slant-front writing desk, burl walnut with satin inlays. Of the period, circa 1700.
$2,400

Wooten

Wooten desk. English Victorian in
walnut and oak. Extra fancy.
$2,600

Wooten desk, desirably smallish,
but simpler and without drawers.
$2,200

American Victorian desk, circa
1880, with swing-out sides in the
Wooten manner. Tambour roll top.
Walnut and oak.
$2,600

FIREPLACE ACCESSORIES

Brass and irons, circa 1770, made
in England.
$250

Wrought-iron and brass andirons,
circa 1880s, in the French manner.
$175

Reproduction brass and irons in
eighteenth-century style.
$85

Egyptian-motif bronze andirons made in France about 1810. Cherub set in background also bronze from same period. Either set . . .
$750

Old reproduction andirons with crystal balls on top. Overtones of French Empire style.
$175

Pair of "old" brass andirons with turned tops, square plinths, cast cabriole legs with ball-and-claw feet. Brass log stops in the same style as the main banisters.
$550

213

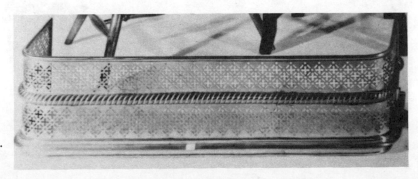

Pierced brass fender in Empire style as seen in U.S. reproduction.
$80

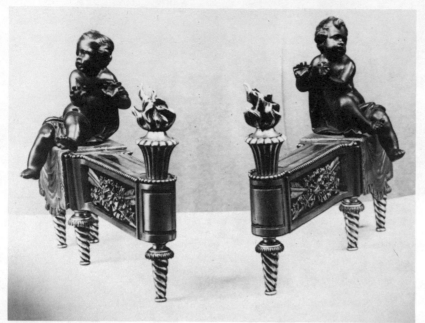

Bronze cherub andirons made in France, circa 1880, in Louis XVI/Directoire style.
$550

Bronze andirons in style of Louis XIV, from Victorian Era in France.
$250

Reproduction of "Federal" wire and brass fireplace fender.
$55

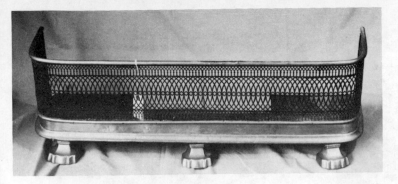

Fireplace fender of cast iron and
brass filigree.
$150

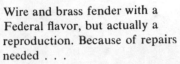

Wire and brass fender with a
Federal flavor, but actually a
reproduction. Because of repairs
needed . . .
$85

Brass bedwarmer was filled with
hot coals and slid between the
blankets.
$225

Same bedwarmer opened.

Brass buckets, depending on size run, available for . . .
$75–$175

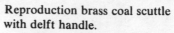

Reproduction brass coal scuttle with delft handle.
$55

Reproduction umbrella stand. Dutch.
$55

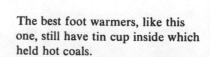

Foot warmers like this, about ten inches square, were made of pine or other hardwood and pierced iron sheets, and were used under foot robes in a carriage, or even indoors in cold rooms. Authentic ones in good condition run up to . . .
$100

The best foot warmers, like this one, still have tin cup inside which held hot coals.

HIGHBOYS

Early American "married" highboy of cherry with good Queen Anne legs and apron.
$4,200

Classical Centennial copy of Philadelphia highboy, made from 1880 to 1930, in cherry and mahogany.
$3,200

American Centennial reproductions of William and Mary highboys in fine figured walnut. Circa 1790. Either one . . .
$2,500

Queen Anne base with duck (or Dutch) feet is married here to a slightly later top. Cherry drawer fronts, maple sides and frame.
$4,000

An all-original matching top and bottom highboy. Definitely in Queen Anne style, but made in America of curly maple. William and Mary finials on apron, but a simple country-made piece, and small for a highboy.
$9,500

"Married" highboy in which Queen Anne base with plain feet is combined with top from a Chippendale (i.e., later) piece. Both pieces have similarly figured maple in drawer fronts, but not matching.
$4,200

218

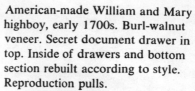
American-made William and Mary highboy, early 1700s. Burl-walnut veneer. Secret document drawer in top. Inside of drawers and bottom section rebuilt according to style. Reproduction pulls.
$1,800

Shells on both top and bottom and bandy legs indicate this highboy to be by Dunlap of New Hampshire. Tiger maple.
$16,500

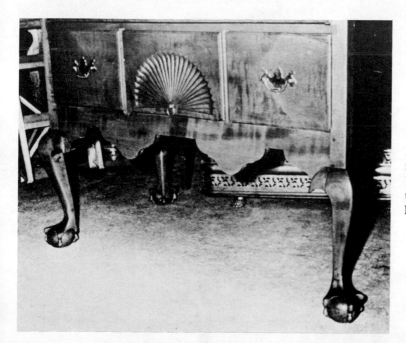

Detail of preceding piece showing firm ball-and-claw foot typical of New England design—as opposed to light and airy version popular in Philadelphia pieces.

Queen Anne maple highboy with flat top from Rhode Island. Removable legs for moving. Fan-carved center drawer. Original brasses.
$9,500

Queen Anne chest on frame—frame later than the top.
$2,800

New England bonnet-top highboy with Queen Anne legs and styling, circa 1740. Cherry. Legs have been heavily restored and bonnet added at later date. Therefore only . . .
$4,500

Twentieth-century copy of flat-topped Queen Anne/George I highboy in mahogany.
$1,600

220

American Queen Anne-style maple highboy. Original cotter-pin-type pulls, chestnut back, etc. Boldly shaped apron. Early 1700s.
$6,500

A married mahogany highboy, but both top and bottom from eighteenth century.
$4,700

Maple highboy with considerable restoration to the base. American-made after Queen Anne style, circa 1750. Because of new legs . . .
$4,500

Highboy with walnut veneers,
made in late 1800s. An American
Centennial, after Massachusetts
styling of Queen Anne style.
$2,800

Fairly modern mahogany highboy.
$1,700

Highboy with walnut veneer
typical of Massachusetts.
Centennial period.
$3,500

222

LAMPS

Hand-carried lantern, circa 1820-style reproduction. Slightly used.
$25

Post lantern of copper, wrought iron, with hollow brass finial. Reproduction.
$125

Partly original and restored post lantern, circa 1890. Of soldered copper.
$250

Heavy cast-metal railroad lamps, often used for outside front-door lights. In the rough (not wired), the pair . . .
$85

Coach lights from a horse-drawn buggy—of soft, cast white metal. Beveled-glass lights. As is and unwired . . .
$260

An unwired gas lamp of case glass (i.e., white inside, dark green outside) on brass base.
$250

Carriage lamp with beveled-glass lights mounted out-of-doors. Wired and restored by soldering, the pair . . .
$250

Victorian milk-glass kerosene lamp with almost-matching replacement shade.
$85

"Gone With the Wind"-type lamp, actually not made until after the Civil War, burned "coal oil" (kerosene). Reproductions are rampant and priced at about half as much as an authentic example such as this . . .
$160

Victorian oil lamp with pressed-glass well and hand-painted base. Wired, replacement shade.
$85

Hand-made post lantern, early 1800s.
$350

Counterweighted hanging Victorian oil lamp with automatic snuffer made of brass, iron, pressed-glass bowl, milk-glass shade.
$200

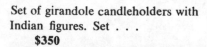

Set of girandole candleholders with Indian figures. Set . . .
$350

Superior counterweighted Victorian hanging oil lamp with hand-decorated well. All original.
$400

All-authentic Victorian hanging
lamp with rare shade.
$250

Common type of Victorian table
lamp with pressed-glass front.
Wired but with parchment
replacement shade.
$85

Banquet-table oil lamp with brass
base weighted with cast iron,
original globe shade, wired.
$185

Blatantly misnamed "Tiffany-type"
lamp. Actually, Vulgar Victorian
of early 1900s. Originally for gas,
now wired.
$200

227

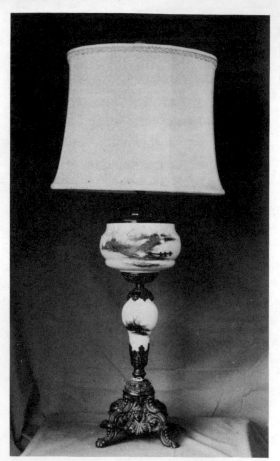

Heavy base of white metal supports well-designed Victorian lamp with Empire heritage. Hand-decorated, wired, with satin shade . . .
$150

Classical student's lamp of brass with green shade.
$280

Victorian pressed-glass oil lamp with matching original top.
$175

Victorian coal-oil lamp with original hand-decorated milk-glass shade.
$200

Lamp made from Chinese vase on stand with satin shade.
$85

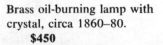 Brass oil-burning lamp with crystal, circa 1860–80.
$450

French art nouveau lamp, signed.
$1,200

French floor lamp of Empire period. Made in late 1800s. Bronze and bronze *doré,* electrified.
$500

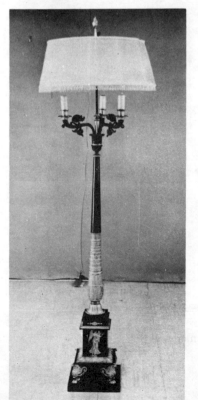

229

Oriental bronze floor lamp.
$400

Pair of candelabra called *lustres,*
crystal, electrified. Brass trees.
Made in the U.S. in the 1920s.
The pair . . .
$500

Cut-glass lamp made in U.S., circa
1900.
$1,200

French vases made into lamps.
Gilded and hand-painted, circa
1810, converted 1922. The
pair . . .
$800

230

Art nouveau table lamp with
bronze stem, made in France, circa
1900.
$675

Bronze banquet-table lamps, made
in France, circa 1880. Each . . .
$350

231

Pink porcelain, etched crystal, and
prisms on gas lamp.
$800

Ballroom chandelier, circa 1900,
four feet in diameter.
$2,200

Bronze Victorian lamp, circa 1900,
in the style of ornateness for its
own sake.
$210

Made-up and electrified floor lamp
of brass and bronze.
$225

LIBRARY FURNISHINGS

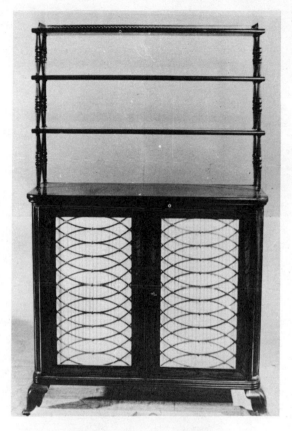

Louis XVI *étagère* made of rosewood about 1840.
$850

Sheraton four-shelf stand of the period in mahogany. Also called whatnot or *étagère*. American origin.
$485

Revolving bookmill. English, circa 1880, in shape of a building. Sign reads: "The True University of These Days." Oak.
$675

Reproduction library steps after
Chippendale design. Fold into end
table. Mahogany and leather.
   $185

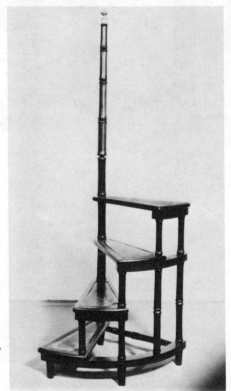

Spiral library steps with brass tip,
hand-tooled leather.
   $185

Pair of Adam looking-glasses, circa 1800, from design book. Gilded gessoed wood and brass. The pair . . .
$3,200

English walnut dressing mirror, circa 1720, Queen Anne style.
$950

Good example of Portuguese Bilbao looking-glass that sailors of early 1800s brought home. Columns are marble, brass, and gilt decoration with five stalks of "wheat" on top.
$2,700

235

Chippendale-style mahogany fretwork looking-glass with eagle of Federal influence. Centennial reproduction.
$165

Queen Anne-style mahogany fretwork looking-glass. Centennial reproduction.
$185

Federal mirror with strong Hepplewhite lines. An awkward eagle, but original nonetheless.
$1,250

American-made convex mirror, circa 1800, with hand-carved eagle on square plinth. Ball-and-leaf decoration, two brass candle branches, original glass in excellent condition. Original gilt finish unretouched and in good condition.
$8,500

Chippendale looking-glass of English origin with phoenix on top. Mahogany, original glass.
$2,500

Hepplewhite mahogany and gilt mirror, English, late 1700s. Of the period. Original glass.
$3,300

Typical example of ogee pine
frame made into mirror. Virtually
mass-produced in late-American
Empire period, they were originally
veneered with dark-red mahogany.
Small . . .
   $75

Chippendale scroll-frame mirror
with some Queen Anne curves.
Depending on size and intricacy of
scrollwork . . .
   $250–$750

An unusual mirror of European
origin, late 1800s.
   $125

Early-American Empire-style mirror, circa 1830, covered with gold-leaf. Usually called Federal, even has thirteen acorns hanging from top. Predecessor of Hitchcock-style mirrors. Twenty-four inches high. Hall mirror.
$220

Hall mirror with thirteen acorns and good reverse-on-glass painting. Beading in vertical columns makes this a Sheraton/Federal style.
$250

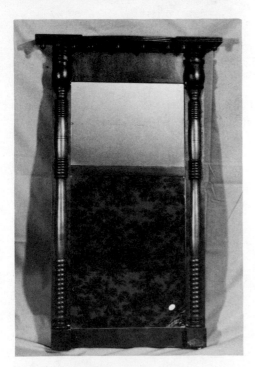

Federal hall mirror in Empire/Federal style. Solid stained mahogany. Would be worth twice as much with original reverse oil painting at top. As is . . .
$100

Oval walnut frame 18 inches high.
$125

238

Moulded pine frame from late
1700s, 24 inches high. Was
originally gesso surface covered
with gilt. Would be worth twice as
much in original condition, but
even as is . . .
  $75

Shaving mirror for man's or lady's
dressing-table mirror of
late-American Empire style.
Mahogany veneer on pine.
  $125

French mirror, gold-leafed, circa
1860–1900, 16 inches wide.
  $400

Gold-leafed period mirror made in
France mid-eighteenth century.
Rests on mantel.
  $1,600

English cheval mirror, circa 1850.
Mahogany, some inlay.
$300

Pair of small gold-leafed mirrors
(26 inches tall) made in England,
circa 1740, Chippendale style.
$2,500

French gold-leafed/green mirror
with scene painted on oval canvas
at top. To hang over mantel.
$750

Ornate gold-leafed pier mirror with
marble-topped console, made in
France 1870. Asymmetric rococo.
$2,800

240

Hall or pier mirror with marble
shelf, gold-leafed carving.
$1,350

Imitation Chippendale/Georgian-
style mirror made in Victorian
England. Mahogany.
$350

American Federal mirror, circa
1810. Gold-leafed, shell carving.
$1,250

Small Federal bull's-eye mirror.
$360

French brass-frame mirror, Victorian reproduction of Louis XV style. (Originally made of wood.)
$200

George I gold-leafed mirror, circa 1715.
$2,750

Painted and gilded Continental mirror.
$150

Eight-foot-tall mirror right out of Chippendale design book, made in mid-1800s.
$2,500

Intricately carved teak cheval mirror made in China, circa 1850, for the English trade.
$2,500

Small mirror (18 inches tall) with etched mirror-glass frame. Made in early 1900s.
$210

243   English dressing piece with full-length swinging cheval mirror made of walnut, circa 1870. Burl-walnut drawer fronts. English Victorian style.
$550

MISCELLANEOUS

Pie cupboard of poplar wood with decoratively pierced metal sheets in doors and on sides for ventilation. Pennsylvania or Ohio origin indicated by wood. Circa 1800.
$650

Southern walnut pie safe on turned feet. Original pierced tin panels, circa 1840.
$675

Hepplewhite pie safe on high legs with original pierced tin panels, from mid-South. Pine, circa 1850s.
$1,100

Cherry hutch or chair-table with
storage box under seat, circa 1780.
Refinished.
$1,100

English Adam-style satinwood
table and display case painted in
the manner of Angelica
Kauffmann.
$1,300

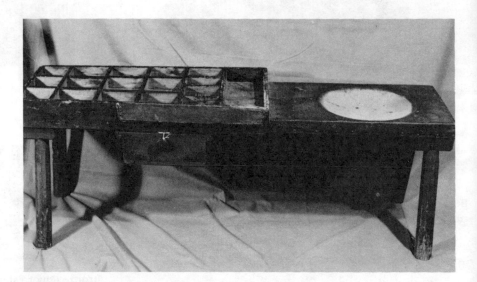

Pine cobbler's bench from Rhode
Island, with original paint and
grime. Circa 1870.
$350

Display table from England in Hepplewhite style, made circa 1820, in satinwood and holly.
$750

Old pine bowl.
$35

Burl-walnut bowl with old repair to rim.
$125

Bronze liquor cabinet in the style of Early Hollywood. Of the period. Marble top.
$1,100

Reproduction copper weathervane. With fake pale-blue paint flaking off, distressed.
$175

Cast-iron horse on a mounting pole used as a trade sign, over 100 years old. Old green paint.
$350

Victorian hanging shelf with house-style doors.
$65

Hepplewhite-style mahogany canterbury of later 1700s. Brass casters. English-made.
$850

Cast white metal warrior, circa 1890.
$85

Wooden bowl used for chopping or letting bread dough rise. Mostly fakes, but even so, if distressing is convincing, depending on size . . .
$35–$75

Country American hanging shelf in pine, circa 1840.
$145

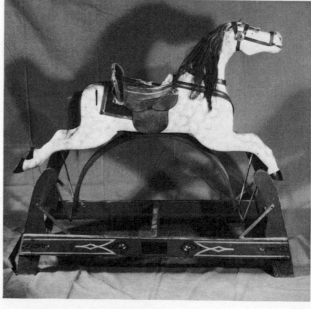

Rocking horse suspended on leather straps, from early 1900s.
$250

Saratoga trunk of pine, originally covered with black leather. Brass binding on bombé shape. Civil War Era and flavor.
$250

Early American flax wheel, circa 1800. Must be complete for modern weavers to pay . . .
$300

Scale from early 1900s, many still in use.
$85

Wicker baby carriage would be
worth almost twice as much with
original parasol. This one, as
is . . .
   $400

Hand-made country-store cabinet,
circa 1900, held small pieces of
hardware. Revolves on pole. As
is . . .
   $500

Gilded cast-iron frame, circa 1890.
American Victorian.
   $85

New England oak cradle.
$150

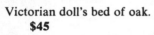

Victorian doll's bed of oak.
$45

Mahogany doll's bed with spool
turnings. Early 1800s.
$85

Pine-based painted mantel of
Federal period with false marble
decoration on top.
$625

Reproduction copper-horse
weathervane.
$175

Reproduction weathervane in
copper with chemically induced
green patina.
$400

Farm table with old red paint on
bottom, worn pine top, drawer.
$325

English gentleman's washstand, or bachelor's commode, with brass basing, tambour bottom, circa 1820. Mahogany.
$1,200

Pair of globes—one celestial, the other terrestrial. Hardwood turned frames. Cook's explorations.
$750

Pair of early American frames in bird's-eye maple.
$150

253

Victorian mahogany shaving stands.
English, 1860-80. Each . . .
   $350

Queen Anne dressing glass on
small ball feet (of the period), and
matching Queen Anne lowboy
(also of the period).
   $1,000 and **$3,000**

American Victorian shaving
stand with white marble top
on mahogany.
   $450

Spinning wheel with heavy turnings
of maple or similar hardwood,
brought to U.S. by Scandinavian
immigrants. Mid-1800s.
   $225

MUSIC-RELATED FURNISHINGS

Victorian rosewood music cabinet
with white marble top.
$1,200

Mahogany music bench with
storage under seat. Victorian-made
Queen Anne.
$175

English Victorian mahogany and
rosewood music cabinet of
devil-may-care design.
$595

Steinway grand piano, circa 1945.
  $3,500

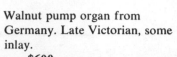

Walnut pump organ from Germany. Late Victorian, some inlay.
  $600

German upright piano with interesting case.
  $750

Grand piano in king, tulip and satinwood, ormolu mounted. In Louis XV style, made circa 1840, rebuilt.
$8,500

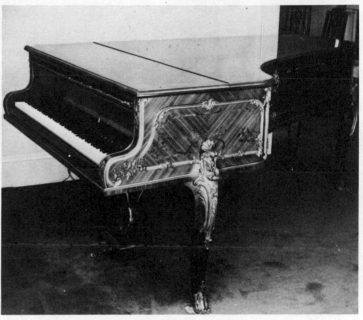

Victorian rosewood music cabinet, circa 1880, with exceptional fretwork.
$1,300

Grand piano painted white in Louis XV style, made 1940.
$2,500

257

Brass music or Bible stand.
Reproduction of Victorian.
$45

Walnut pump organ from England.
$550

Music stand in dark ebony from
Victorian England.
$650

258

ORIENTAL FURNISHINGS

Cabinet on stand in styles ranging from pre-Queen Anne to Georgian chinoiserie. Dark-red lacquer.
$650

Excellent example of teak parlor cabinet with ivory inlays. Made in China for the English market, circa 1830.
$2,400

Chinese commode, mid-1800s.
$1,200

Lacquered Chinese display cabinet
with raised figures, no great age.
$825

Black lacquered oriental
Coromandel commode with
painted decoration.
$275

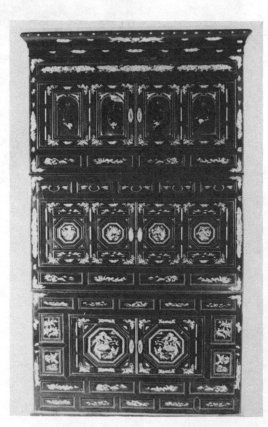

Drop-front desk from China, circa
1840, made of elm, front
lacquered.
$675

Small dovetailed Korean wall-front
cabinet with brass corners and
hinges. Secret lock.
   $400

Authentic Korean chests, circa
1840, made of teak and figured
elm, sometimes mother-of-pearl,
decorative brass hinges. Each . . .
   $1,200

Antique Korean cabinet made of
teak with mother-of-pearl inlay,
made about 1850.
   $2,200

PARLOR SETS

Aubusson tapestry with blue background on Louis XVI parlor set of four armchairs and one sofa.
$5,500

John Henry Belter parlor set of carved laminated rosewood. Around . . .
$23,000

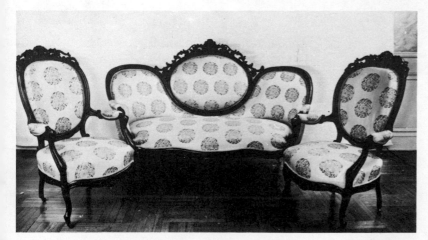

American Victorian parlor set of mahogany in the Belter manner.
$1,600

262

American Victorian sofa and
matching chair.
$1,100

American Victorian. Of walnut in
the Eastlake style. Set . . .
$850

Louis XVI-style Aubusson-covered
salon set made in 1870.
$2,200

Belter parlor set, laminated
rosewood carving.
$12,000

Four Belter chairs with grape
carvings.
$5,500

Set of Belter chairs in laminated
rosewood, but not ornately carved.
$4,200

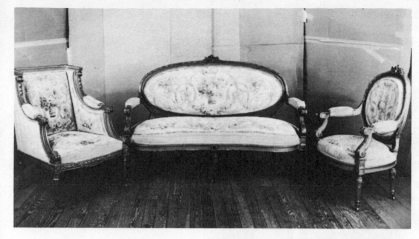

Louis XVI pieces with Aubusson covering. All three . . .
$2,850

Cast-iron garden set, circa 1900.
$650

Highly gilded and carved salon set, made about 1870 in France in Louis XV style.
$4,200

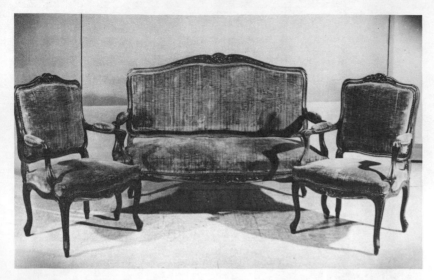

Walnut Louis XV-style sofa and
two chairs.
   $2,300

Three matching Belter pieces
without pierced carving. Solid
mahogany instead of laminated
rosewood.
   $4,500

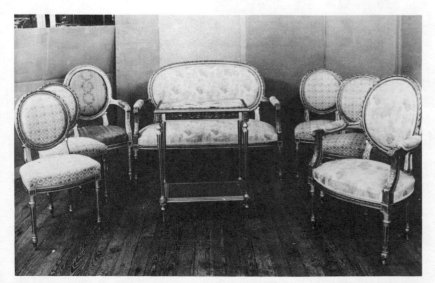

Louis XVI salon set with table,
made circa 1900. Somewhere?
Factory workmanship.
   $2,500

266

Two ballroom chairs and window bench in Louis XV style, made circa 1880.
$750

Unusual quality pair of Belter chairs in laminated rosewood, grape carving.
$6,500

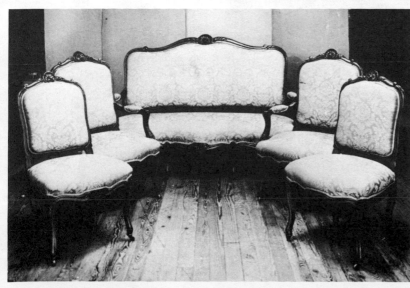

Five-piece gilded Louis XV salon set made in Victorian Era.
$3,200

SCREENS

Pole or fire screen, adjustable in height, late 1700s. Embroidered, but with Queen Anne snake feet. Mahogany.
$450

Needlepoint screen in mahogany frame with arched top, mahogany pole-and-tripod base with rat-claw feet. Early 1800s.
$350

Victorian fire screen in mahogany with ornate carving.
$140

Coromandel screen in dark-red
lacquer decorated on both sides.
$700

Chinese mid-1800s screen with
applied mother-of-pearl,
teakwood, Coromandel lacquered
panels.
$2,200

Coromandel screen, dark-red
lacquer with insets of jade and
other stones.
$1,500

Coromandel screen, circa 1770,
from China.
   $4,500

Painted French screen for the
parlor.
   $1,100

SECRETARIES

Pine secretary, circa 1850, in
basically late American Empire
with Gothic Revival influence as
seen in arches. An interesting
transitional piece. Refinished . . .
$900

Same secretary opened.

Twentieth-century reproduction of
ornate Chippendale-style secretary
with carved base and ogee bracket
feet. Mahogany veneered.
$2,300

Empire secretary. Originally
veneered with mahogany. Stripped
down here to pine, stained Early
American brown and finished.
Circa 1850.
$900

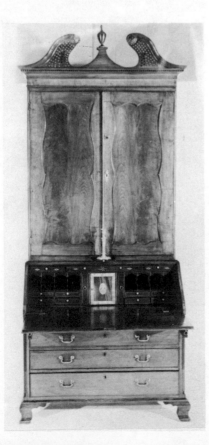

Early American walnut
secretary-bookcase with mahogany
trim, ogee bracket feet, pediment
wings ending in carved rosettes,
eagle inlay on inside door. Candle
slide centered under doors. Circa
1776. Philadelphia origin.
$14,000

272

Curly maple and cherry linen press of American origin in Hepplewhite style with French feet, inlaid drawers. Circa late 1700s.
$3,500

Hepplewhite desk in cherry and maple. Bookcase top of Empire lines was added later.
$2,500

Primitive piece from a country post office. Late 1800s. Pine.
$1,250

Oxbow-front, slant-front desk with bookcase top, made in Massachusetts. Original brass pulls, old glass, ogee bracket feet, figured mahogany. Faithful Chippendale.
$12,500

Continental secretary lavishly inlaid and veneered after Adam, made in mid-1800s.
$1,850

English Victorian secretary-bookcase, circa 1880. Top drawer falls down to make writing surface. Mahogany with carving. Design combines various earlier English and French styles.
$1,350

274

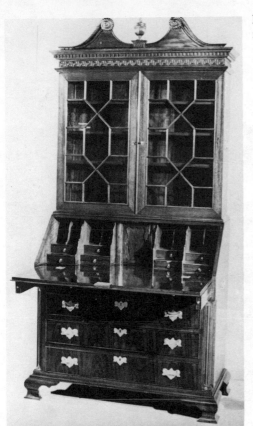

Edwardian secretary reproduction
made in England.
$2,200

English mahogany
bookcase-secretary with slide that
pulls out to make writing surface.
In Hepplewhite style of 1760–70
with classical Chippendale
fretwork top and feet. Just the kind
of piece for which the term
"Georgian" was invented.
$1,800

275

English 1780 secretary-bookcase in
the Hepplewhite manner. Top
drawer front comes down to make
writing surface. Light flame
mahogany.
$3,200

Dutch walnut veneer secretary,
style of 1760–80.
$3,500

American Federal piece made circa
1810. French Empire design
elements, solid and veneer
mahogany.
$3,500

276

American Hepplewhite secretary
with eagle inlay, circa 1790.
$4,500

George III/Hepplewhite secretary made in England, 1780.
$3,500

American Empire secretary made 1830 with Louis XV carving on doors and top. Very unusual.
$2,500

Small walnut secretary in the Queen Anne manner, made about 1890–1900 in England.
$1,500

Padouk mahogany secretary made in India for the English trade, circa 1770. Gilded s-curve broken pediment. Rare piece.
$11,500

George III broken-arch pediment with blind fretwork, mahogany. Good example.
$6,000

Drop-front Victorian English walnut secretary.
$650

Late-Georgian secretary made circa 1790, classical Adam influence.
$8,500

Reproduction George III secretary made in England.
$1,400

Dutch bombé secretary made circa 1760, figured walnut.
$5,000

Chinese desk in red lacquer, made in late 1800s.
$1,450

American Empire secretary made in 1840.
$850

Double-dome walnut Queen Anne secretary made in 1720.
$10,500

Mahogany Hepplewhite secretary,
circa 1780. Satinwood interior and
inlay.
$3,500

American Victorian walnut
secretary.
$1,400

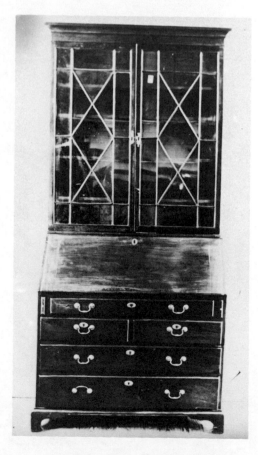

George III mahogany secretary,
circa 1770.
$3,500

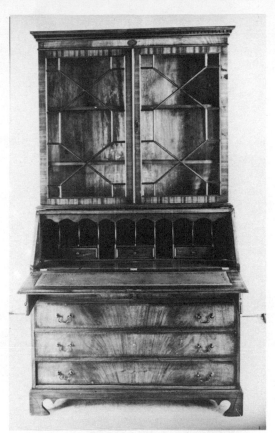

American-made reproduction of a George II secretary in mahogany veneer.
$1,500

Narrow Edwardian secretary of mahogany with rosewood and satinwood inlay.
$1,800

American Victorian secretary in transitional Empire/Gothic style, circa 1770.
$1,400

Empire into Gothic American
Victorian secretary, circa 1860.
$1,200

Georgian/Hepplewhite secretary,
circa 1780, in mahogany with
fall-front top drawer to open desk.
$3,500

Actually a bookcase commode.
The Hepplewhite base with French
feet is the best half of this unhappy
marriage, as central finial is missing
from broken-arch pediment.
However, use of cherry indicates
American origin.
$2,200.

282

SETTEES/LOVE SEATS

George I or Queen Anne settee
with pad feet in walnut.
   $3,200

Early 1900s version of a Queen
Anne settee. In walnut with pad
feet, needlepoint covering.
   $1,200

Walnut settle dated 1679 but made
in late 1800s. Storage seat.
   $1,100

Victorian version Chippendale
settee in mahogany.
$1,250

Carved teakwood settee made in
the 1850s in China.
$1,350

Louis XVI settee made in 1880s.
$900

284

French Provincial settee made of walnut, gilded.
$2,600

French Provincial settee of walnut.
$950

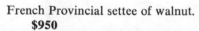

Classical Adam triple-back settee, painted satinwood. Made 1770s.
$3,500

Louis XV tête-à-tête love seat
made in Victorian Era.
   $850

English Victorian settee in
gussied-up Chippendale style.
   $1,000

Walnut settle made in early 1700s.
   $1,600

Fine example of George I or
Queen Anne settee. Burl walnut,
double back, made about 1730.
$7,500

Louis XVI-style daybed, made in
late 1800s, gilded.
$950

Double shield-back Hepplewhite
settee made and painted in 1790.
$1,500

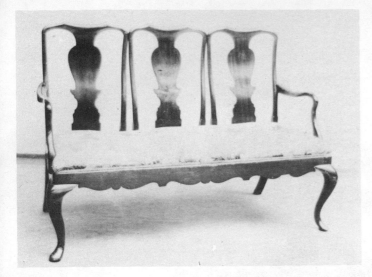

Triple-back mahogany settee made in 1880s. By-the-book Queen Anne style.
$1,350

American Victorian settee, circa 1860, with valuable petit-point.
$1,250

Ormolu mounted Empire settee, circa 1810, in mahogany.
$1,200

George I settee made of
mahogany, circa 1715.
$2,200

Queen Anne-style triple-back settee
in walnut with cane in backs,
William and Mary back tops.
$1,100

Very Louis XV Victorian settee
made in England of rosewood.
$2,200

289

Victorian attempt to reproduce
Louis XV style, gilded.
    $800

Victorian reproduction of Louis
XVI.
    $850

SIDEBOARDS

Simple English serving table with square legs in oak, with replacement brasses. Late 1700s.
$650

English Victorian reproduction of Hepplewhite sideboard with inlaid veneer. Oxbow or serpentine front. Bell-flower inlay on top of tapered legs.
$1,450

Oak sideboard of Jacobean to William and Mary period, geometric mouldings. Bail pulls inappropriate, should be pendants.
$2,850

English Victorian reproduction Hepplewhite sideboard with fine tapered legs and spade feet, oxbow front.
$650

Southern hunt board of hard pine for serving men on horses. Circa 1800. Not as tall as usual.
$1,200

English sideboard, circa 1810. Sheraton, mahogany veneer. Bottle drawers.
$1,600

American Hepplewhite server in
dark mahogany. Two doors below.
$1,300

American Hepplewhite mahogany
sideboard with oval inlays.
$3,600

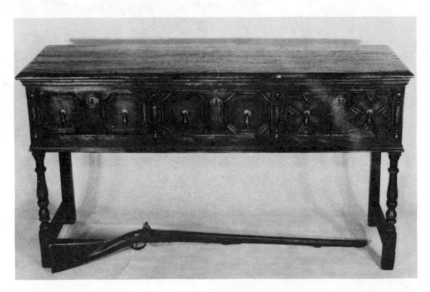

293

Jacobean oak dresser base, now
sideboard with original pulls. Early
1700s.
$1,900

Very Adam sideboard made true to
his drawing, circa 1830. Light
mahogany and satinwood.
$4,000

Welsh oak dresser, made in that
country about 1750.
$2,500

English Victorian copy of
a Hepplewhite bow-front sideboard
in flaming mahogany veneers.
Spade feet.
$2,200

Hepplewhite sideboard with inlaid fan shelves, mahogany and satinwood inlays. Circa 1790.
$2,700

Hepplewhite mahogany and satinwood inlaid sideboard.
$2,300

Hepplewhite sideboard with brass rail and spade feet, but less desirable wide size.
$1,800

English Victorian version of a Chippendale sideboard.
$700

Mahogany Hepplewhite sideboard, made circa 1790–1800.
$2,300

Tambour-top sideboard with built-in knife boxes, made in England circa 1770. George III/Hepplewhite. Very rare.
$6,000

296

Welsh dresser country-made, circa 1760, with mahogany and satinwood inlays.
$2,600

English Regency sideboard with paw feet and lion-head pulls, knife urns on either end. Circa 1810.
$1,800

Small four-legged Hepplewhite sideboard, nicely inlaid.
$1,700

Hepplewhite mahogany sideboard
with bowed front and unusual
double spade feet.
$2,400

Welsh oak dresser, circa 1900.
$1,000

298

American Victorian parlor cabinet,
walnut applied carving, circa 1860.
$2,300

Brass-rail sideboard, circa 1790.
Spade feet, mahogany, etc.
$2,500

Reeded legs on this sideboard
make it transitional between
Hepplewhite and Sheraton styles.
Circa 1780s.
$1,900

Second Empire sideboard in
rosewood, ormolu mounted.
$1,400

Continental demilune sideboard
with fancy inlay, marble top, made
1890s. (Austrian?)
   $1,800

Demilune sideboard, Hepplewhite,
in dark mahogany, with spade feet.
Circa 1770.
   $2,000

SOFAS

Federal-style sofa upholstered in blue velvet with rolled arms. Mahogany frame well carved. An American Centennial piece.
$850

Transitional Chippendale (back) to Hepplewhite sofa with eight tapered legs on brass casters and upholstered in gold brocade. Centennial, circa 1890.
$850

American Empire sofa, straight-backed and scrolled ams, considerable fine carving on front. Circa 1840.
$1,800

Centennial Sheraton sofa with well-detailed carving, correct proportions. Circa 1890.
$900

Chippendale-style Centennial sofa.
$750

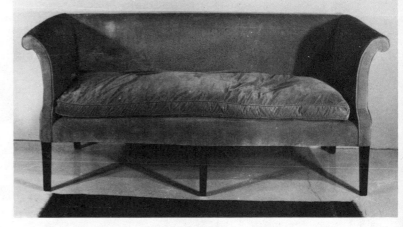

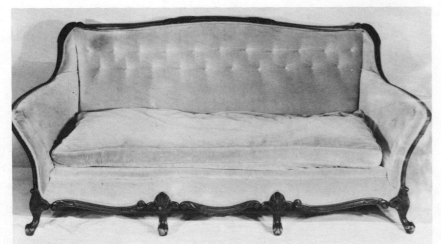

American Victorian sofa, circa 1850, after the French style of Louis XV.
$1,400

302

English mahogany frame sofa in
Regency style.
$1,250

Massachusetts Sheraton sofa, circa
1815, with straight back.
$2,300

Loose-seat Massachusetts Sheraton
sofa with scroll arm. Mahogany.
$2,700

French Victorian sofa made in
1860s of gilded mahogany.
$600

French Empire daybed-sofa with
ormolu mounts. For posing on in
long gowns. Early 1800s. Fabric
gone.
$950

Louis XV walnut sofa reproduced
in France, circa 1870.
$850

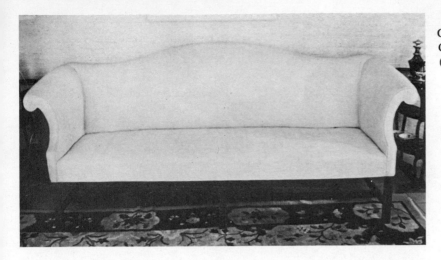

Camel-back mahogany sofa with Chippendale straight legs (Marlborough). George II, 1750.
$2,300

American Empire window bench of pillar-and-scroll period, 1880s. Mahogany veneer on block pine.
$450

Camel-back sofa with French cabriole legs, made in England, circa 1870.
$1,400

American Federal or early-Empire sofa in the manner of Duncan Phyfe, early 1800s. Winged claw foot.
$2,600

Sheraton reeded leg on casters in mahogany. Of the period.
$2,500

Louis XV walnut sofa, circa 1870.
$900

306

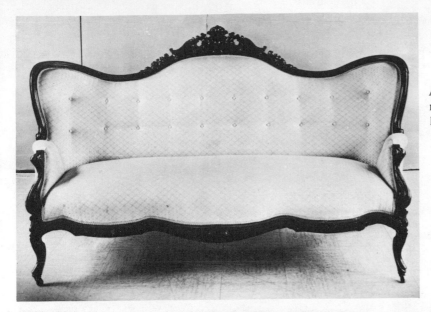

American Victorian carved rosewood settee, circa 1860, with light Louis XV lines.
$1,300

Hepplewhite camel-back sofa.
$2,500

Fine Belter settee from a parlor set, with grape carving in laminated rosewood.
$4,500

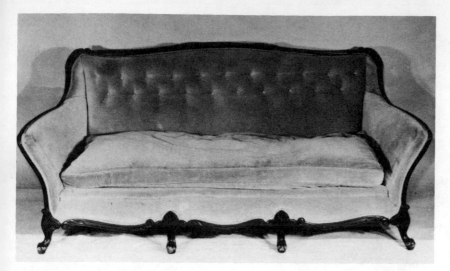

American Victorian sofa, with
regrettably attached French legs.
$500

American Victorian sofa or love
seat in walnut, circa 1860.
$850

American Victorian settee with
Louis XVI-inspired legs and Sèvres
plaque in center of top. Walnut.
$1,200

308

Good example of Chesterfield sofa of tufted leather. A modern reproduction. (The leather on originals has rotted beyond repair.) English Victorian Era.
$1,400

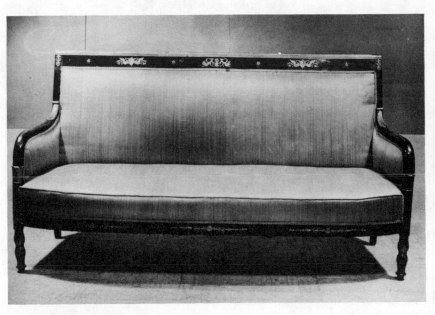

French Empire sofa with delicate ormolu bronze mounting on ebonized wood.
$1,800

Fine camel-back sofa of classical Chippendale design. Marlborough legs. Made in U.S. around 1900.
$1,500

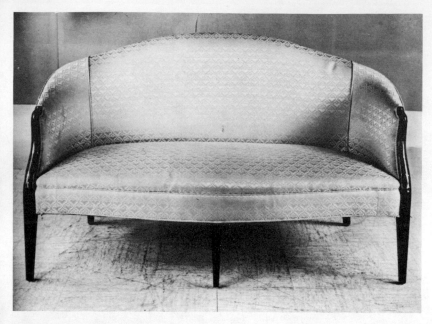

Small mahogany settee or love seat
in the Hepplewhite style made in
Victorian Era.
   $950

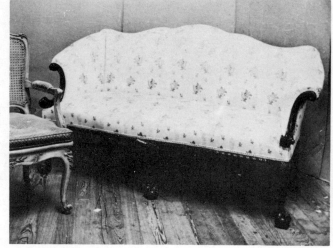

Victorianized Chippendale sofa.
      $1,300

American Victorian walnut sofa
under the influence of Louis XV.
      $1,250

310

American Victorian Belter-style
sofa of carved laminated rosewood.
$3,600

STOOLS

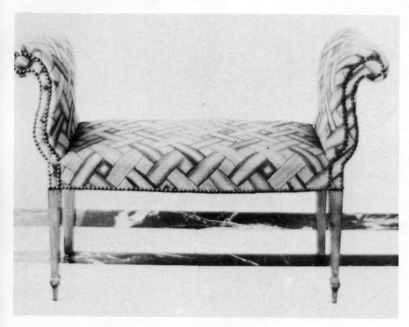

Window bench, circa 1780,
Hepplewhite.
$950

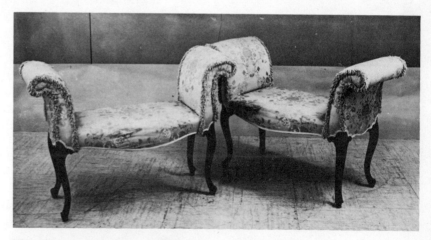

Victorian-made pair of window
benches. Made in England after
Louis XV style.
$750

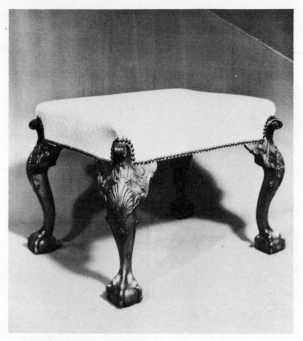

Chippendale stool with fine
carving. Mahogany with scroll top
and shell carving.
$1,750

Queen Anne-style walnut stool
with pad feet. Reproduction, circa
1900.
$250

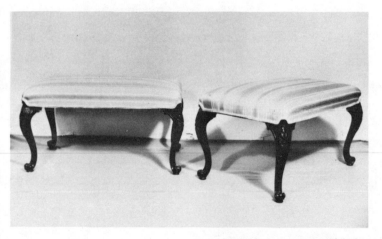

Pair of window benches with fine
1780-style legs—Chippendale.
Good Victorian reproductions.
$1,200

313

TABLES

Bedside

Very American maple end table of
early 1800s made in great
numbers. Sheraton inspiration.
Very strong.
   $175

Striped-maple Sheraton table,
made in U.S., circa 1840.
   $650

Sheraton bedside table with turned
legs in maple. Mahogany drawer
fronts. American.
   $250

Country-made American pine night table with tapered legs of Hepplewhite. Circa early 1800s.
$175

American bedside table with veneered mahogany drawer front of Empire period, circa 1880. The rest, pine and poplar stained to match mahogany veneer.
$125

Two-drawer bedside table. American Sheraton with ample front drawers.
$260

Country-made American Sheraton two-drawer bedside table of cherry.
$175

Mahogany nightstand imported
from England, circa 1860.
$150

Mahogany Sheraton-style
two-drawer nightstand with fluted
legs and serpentine front.
Cock-beaded drawers in light
wood.
$350

Fine early-American Sheraton
table, circa 1750. In mahogany
with flame satinwood drawer fronts
and cookie corners, reed legs.
$475

Sheraton night table with maple
and mahogany drawer fronts, the
rest maple.
$245

Candlestand

Candlestand with snake-foot pedestal and square top with recessed round corners, in cherry. American, circa mid-1700s. Unfortunately, top is replacement.
$250

Queen Anne-style butternut-wood candlestand with snake feet. From New England, early 1700s. All original.
$375

Octagonal-top candlestand in tiger maple.
$225

Candlestand with Hepplewhite
curule or saber leg in maple, circa
1830.
   $185

Candlestand from New England in
Hepplewhite manner with spade
feet on crabfoot legs. Unusual.
   $325

318

Crabfoot Hepplewhite/Sheraton
candlestand from New England in
cherry or maple.
   $275

Queen Anne-looking candlestand in maple with strong snake feet.
$700

Wrought-iron leg strengtheners on this table are original, and no antique tripod table is authentic without them.

Card

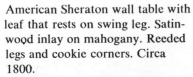

American Sheraton wall table with leaf that rests on swing leg. Satin-wood inlay on mahogany. Reeded legs and cookie corners. Circa 1800.
$900

American Hepplewhite card table with leaf; supported by swinging leg. Inlaid Adam urns on leg tops. 1790–1810.
$2,500

American Empire table of mahogany veneer on pine with lyre base. Top lifts up to open and swivels around for support to make card table. Late 1800s.
$225

Sheraton game table with fold-back
top in mahogany. American.
$1,100

George I/Queen Anne card table
with top that opens and swivels to
rest on two swinging legs. Made
circa 1710.
$2,500

Sheraton game table with fold-back
top in mahogany. American.
$1,100

Chippendale-style gaming table
made in Victorian England.
$1,200

Sheraton mahogany card table.
Swing leg supports flip-over cover.
Reeded and turreted legs,
serpentine inlaid apron. Edges of
tops are inlaid and cross-banded.
$750

Chippendale card table with
authentic-looking carving. Made
about 1870 in England.
$1,200

Victorian oak center table
combining French and Georgian
ideas.
$700

American Victorian center table
made of rosewood with white
marble top.
$450

Scandinavian-made center table
with Egyptian motifs of the French
Empire style. Fruitwood.
$3,000

English Victorian reproduction of
Chippendale library table.
Mahogany.
$850

Center table with onyx marble top.
Gilded, French Victorian.
$1,200

324

Irish Chippendale center table in
mahogany, circa 1770.
$2,500

Jacobean-style walnut refectory or
library table. Victorian
reproduction.
$1,200

English Victorian reproduction of
"Georgian" table. Mahogany.
$1,200

Louis XV center table with inlaid chessboard and fine satinwood, etc. inlays. Ormolu mounted. Circa 1870.
$1,800

Victorian center table in hard dark mahogany.
$850

English Victorian card table in mahogany, circa 1880.
$600

326

American Victorian marble top in walnut. Renaissance style.
$400

French *bureau-plat,* or writing table, in 1770 style of rococo Louis XV. Ormolu mounted, pale wood inlays, leather top. Made in France in late 1800s.
$4,500

Boulle center table with brass and tortoise shell laid into the wood. Made in France, circa 1880.
$1,600

Satinwood two-tier table made in
England, circa 1790. Hepplewhite.
$700

Chippendale piecrust table in
mahogany. Centennial.
$1,500

Oval American Empire center
table.
$400

328

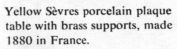

Yellow Sèvres porcelain plaque table with brass supports, made 1880 in France.
$1,350

Cloissoné-topped brass table made in China in mid-1800s for British market.
$750

Victorian Renaissance marble-top table. Walnut.
$350

Glass-topped mahogany display table in the Victorian style of a little bit of everything.
$450

English Victorian foul-up of Chippendale tripod table design. 1900.
$350

Classical French Empire table in rosewood, English version, circa 1830. Called Regency style.
$650

A Sèvres plaque table of the Queen and her court, circa 1780. Heavy ormolu base. Louis XVI rococo.
$10,000

Regency two-part table with center
leaf, made in England in early
1800s.
$2,000

Early twentieth-century
reproduction in mahogany.
$1,000

American Empire banquet table
with two extra-wide leaves,
rope-twist legs. Mahogany. Circa
1860.
$1,200

Sheraton dining or banquet table
in two parts with center leaf.
Mahogany with reeded legs and
brass casters. American, circa
1800.
$1,500

French Provincial refectory table
with slide-out leaves. Walnut,
inlaid top.
$1,400

Double-pedestal dining table from the English Regency period in approximate Sheraton style. Mahogany, extra leaves.
$4,000

Concertina-action table made in England, circa 1800. Mahogany.
$3,200

Concertina table closed.

333

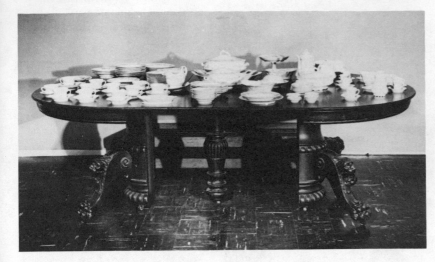

American Victorian expandable dining table in dark oak.
$950

Three-part dining table has swing-leg drop-leaf table in center, matching demilune consoles here placed at ends. Hepplewhite, spade feet. Of the period.
$3,300

Triple-pedestal table of George III period, Sheraton style. Of the period.
$3,500

334

Rococo Louis XV dining table with top that opens to take an unfinished leaf. Made in Victorian Era.
$1,400

Three-part mahogany table with fourteen legs. Hepplewhite. Mahogany.
$2,400

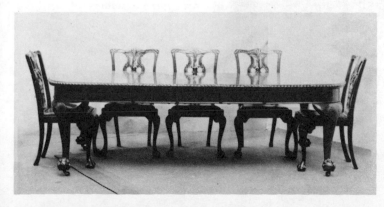

English Victorian table in the Chippendale style. Mahogany.
$1,600

Drop-leaf

Primitive pine table with tapered
Hepplewhite legs is earlier than
those with turned legs. Late 1700s.
Scraped and waxed in Canadian
manner.
$250

American cherry table of Sheraton
flavor, circa 1780–90. Refinished
bargain at . . .
$350

336

Country drop-leaf table with pine boards and irregularly turned maple legs. Circa 1850, from balls on feet. As is . . .
$150

French mahogany table in Louis XVI style with four drop-leaves and bountiful inlays. Made in Victorian Era.
$1,200

Refinished drop-leaf pine table with very wide leaf supported by swing legs. From mid-1800s. Would be worth twice as much in cherry, but in pine . . .
$400

Queen Anne pad-foot dining table, made circa 1710, in mahogany.
$1,800

English wake table in mahogany with Marlborough legs, circa 1780
$2,400

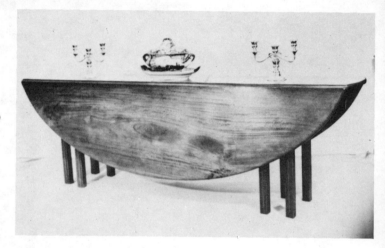

Drop-leaf table from early period of American Empire, 1830–50. Acanthus-leaf carving on legs and cherry top, which should be stained darker to match legs.
$275

338

Queen Anne table with drawer, in mahogany. Victorian-made.
$1,200

Queen Anne oval dining table with swing legs. Walnut, circa 1730.
$1,700

Spider gate-leg table, mahogany, circa 1780.
$1.800

Long-leaf drop-leaf table, circa
1780, George II/Chippendale style.
Mahogany.
  $1,400

Jacobean gate-leg table made about
1690.
  $1,400

George III table with reeded legs,
long mahogany leaves.
  $1,400

Jacobean gate-leg table in oak,
circa 1690.
$1,200

Spider-leg table, circa 1780, with
pad feet, dark mahogany.
$1,200

Six-legged long-leaf table with
reeded legs. Circa 1800, English.
Mahogany.
$1,200

Cherry drop-leaf table with swing leg, made circa 1800. Country-made.
$2,000

English gate-leg wake table. Walnut. Early 1700s.
$2,200

Cherry drop-leaf table with straight cabriole legs and Queen Anne feet. Late 1700s, New England.
$2,200

342

Slipper-foot table from Rhode
Island in mahogany with base,
circa 1750, but top is an old
replacement.
$1,500

Occasional

Rosewood-based architect's table,
circa 1815. Regency/Sheraton.
$1,800

Hepplewhite architect's table with
leather top glued on drawing
surface.
$900

Butler's tray on stand. If of the
period, up to . . .
$850

344

Beau Brummel gentleman's dressing table of the Hepplewhite period in mahogany.
$650

American architect's stand in mahogany. Centennial origin.
$350

Small, delicate schoolmaster's desk of pine. Sheraton feeling. Mid-1800s.
$300

Louis XVI-style side table, gilded and with marble top.
$1,400

Victorian vintage trays in the
Georgian manner mounted on new
stands to serve as coffee tables.
Each . . .
   $250

Richly inlaid Dutch dressing table
with barley-twist legs. Circa 1710.
   $1,110

346

Set of Victorian-made nesting
tables in late-Georgian manner.
Mahogany and inlaid tops.
   $400

Sophisticated English rosewood table with ormolu mounted pedestals. Made circa 1880 in England after the French. The pair . . .
$800

Kidney-shaped English writing table, circa 1800, Regency/Sheraton, mahogany.
$600

Pair of occasional tables in William and Mary style, painted, factory-made, circa 1920. The pair . . .
$200

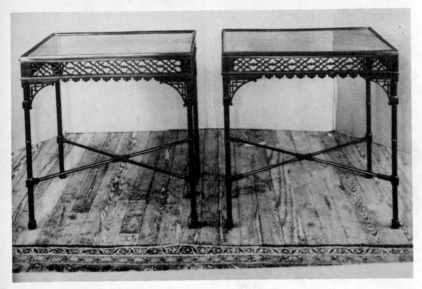

Pair of display tables made in
England, circa 1780. Slightly
Chippendale design with mahogany
fretwork. Called silver tables.
Mahogany. Rare. The pair . . .
   $2,700

Teak pedestal with rouge marble
top. Made in China, circa 1850, for
the English market.
   $500

French Empire-style pedestal table.
Victorian reproduction.
   $350

348

Satinwood occasional tables, made
1880 after Adam drawings.
Each . . .
   $200

Teak stand made in China, circa
1850, for English market.
   $250

Pembroke

Hepplewhite pembroke table with
inlay and cross-banding of ankles.
Circa 1790. English origin.
$950

Nicely inlaid Hepplewhite
pembroke table of the period.
American.
$1,600

American primitive table with
scrubbed top and splayed legs in
pine. Circa 1850.
$400

American pembroke table with
serpentine leaf, circa 1780, in
Chippendale style, mahogany.
$2,800

Pembroke table with drawer, circa
1790. Hepplewhite legs, straight
English leaf.
$850

Sewing

American Sheraton sewing table with bag that slides out with bottom-drawer frame. Rope-carved legs and brass casters. Circa 1820.
    $450

Small worktable with Sheraton rope legs and cookie corners, ivory inlays at keyholes. Mahogany, solid and veneer.
    $350

American Empire sewing or worktable. Refinished to reveal fat pine legs.
$225

American Empire lyre-base table of pillar-and-scroll period. Mahogany veneer on pine.
$175

Early-American Empire worktable (or sewing table) on pedestal stand. Stylistically excellent.
$350

Late-Sheraton two-drawer table with rope-carved legs, maple drawer fronts.
$285

Sewing table, English, circa 1830,
fine mahogany veneer.
$650

Two-drawer and two-leaf
mahogany Sheraton worktable (or
sewing table). Turned legs and
brass casters. English-made, circa
1800.
$450

Sheraton sewing table, circa 1800,
from England. Mahogany.
$850

Valley of Virginia hunt board with
fine tapered legs in hard pine.
$1,400

English lowboy in walnut and
walnut veneer of the Queen Anne
period.
$3,300

355

Walnut side table, circa 1750,
country-made after Queen Anne.
$950

Hepplewhite mahogany side table.
$500

Dresser base, circa 1720, with evened feet, lacquered, inlaid floral design. Queen Anne period.
$1,500

Hepplewhite mahogany demilune side table. Of the period.
$900

French ladies' dressing table circa 1870. Top flips up to reveal mirror on other side. Louis XV rococo.
$700

Bureau-plat, or writing table, in good Louis XV style, made in Victorian France.
$1,700

Hepplewhite console table with spade feet, inlaid mahogany.
$750

Marble top, rosewood dressing
table in Louis XV Victorian style.
Circa 1840. American.
$1,400

Rosewood American Victorian
dressing table with marble top
after Louis XV.
$1,250

358

American Victorian server for dining-room set. Rosewood with grape carving. Close to Belter in style.
$2,400

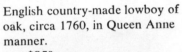

English country-made lowboy of oak, circa 1760, in Queen Anne manner.
$850

Mahogany console table with mahogany marquetry top. After Chippendale but Victorian made.
$1,300

Triple-top mahogany table in
Chinese/Chippendale design.
Opens to make tea, card, and
dining tables. Of the period.
$2,000

Highboy base of the Queen Anne
period, but awkward legs.
$1,500

Stretcher

American country-made stretcher
table of mid-1800s.
$385

Pine tavern table with scrubbed
top, early 1800s.
$800

Splay-leg tavern table with turned legs and rectangular stretchers. Butterfly leaf supports. New England circa 1750s.
$6,500

Pine hanging cupboard and pine stretcher table, circa 1850s, U.S. Either one . . .
$250

American stretcher or tavern table. Maple turned legs and button feet. Single long drawer. New England origin. One-piece top with breadboard ends. Circa 1750.
$1,200

Early 1700s American tavern table
with splayed maple legs and
stretchers. Two-board pine top
with maple breadboard ends.
Button feet. Full-length drawer
with slanted ends. Old brass knob.
Top looks good, but is probably
not original.
   $1,100

Tea

Victorian marble-topped stand of Renaissance style, refinished. Small size.
$150

American Queen Anne tray-top tea table in cherry, circa 1750s.
$11,000

English mahogany gallery table with octagonal top, circa 1780.
$850

Tea table of Irish origin, circa
1750, cabriole legs and unusual
feet. Dish top and shaped apron.
Called Irish Chippendale, but
actually developed independently
in Ireland.
     $4,500

American Queen Anne tea table in
figured maple.
     $2,400

Tilt-top

American Hepplewhite tilt-top
table in cherry. Queen Anne
feeling in snake-footed legs.
    $385

Detail of tilting and locking
mechanism of same table.

Close-up of birdcage.

Large tripod table (four-foot diameter) with snake feet in mahogany. Circa 1750.
$825

Same table from behind, showing birdcage device that allows table to both turn and tilt.

English oval breakfast table, made
circa 1780. Sheraton legs and brass
paw casters. Mahogany.
   $1,800

Walnut tilt-top mahogany table
with birdcage, rimmed top typical
of Delaware Valley. Heavy snake
feet. Circa 1750.
   $4,000

English tea table with tilt-top and
birdcage tilt-and-turn device in
mahogany. Dish top. Circa 1850.
   $650

368

English piecrust table, circa 1750,
with Queen Anne legs. Mahogany.
$1,500

American dish-top tea table in
mahogany with heavy snake feet,
circa 1780.
$1,000

Piecrust table, circa 1780. Paw
feet, acanthus-leaf carving,
mahogany. Pristine condition.
Chippendale.
$1,700

Chippendale piecrust table, 1760s.
$1,500

Custom-made piecrust tea table
with tilt-top in mahogany. Legs are
too straight, snake feet too heavy.
$165

Writing

Custom-made writing table in the Hepplewhite style, inlaid, but wood inappropriately stained dark mahogany.
   $350

Bonheur du jour, or French ladies' writing table, Louis XVI, rosewood and brass. Made in France in 1870.
   $850

Custom-made Hepplewhite-style writing desk with inlay lines, brass casters.
   $650

Writing table with bookcase,
French Second Empire, circa 1815,
rosewood, ormolu mounts.
$750

Victorian-made ladies' writing
desk, lacquered with William and
Mary trumpet legs.
$750

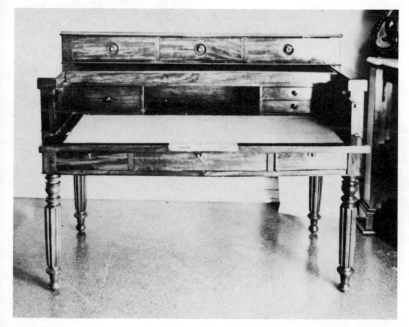

Mahogany piano desk made in
England 1840. Empire with
Victorian legs.
$600

French Empire bonheur du jour
with Sèvres plaques, brass rails,
ebonized wood, inlaid.
$3,250

Louis XVI ebonized writing desk
covered with ormolu and Sèvres
plaques. Made in 1880s in France.
$2,500

French cylinder desk made of
kingwood, circa 1870. Marble top.
$1,500

373

Ladies' dressing table of satinwood made after an Adam drawing, decorated in the style of Angelica Kauffmann. Made circa 1875.
$1,400

Small Welsh dresser made of oak.
$1,200

Second Empire French writing table or bonheur du jour. Ebonized wood, ormolu, Sèvres plaques, brass galleries. Made 1840.
$2,500

374

English Carlton mahogany desk,
circa 1780, Hepplewhite design.
$3,500

Satinwood curio case after Adam
design. Made circa 1780.
$1,450

375

Louis XV bonheur du jour with
vernis martin panels, ormolu
mounts. Made 1870.
$1,400

WARDROBES
AND ARMOIRES

Press cupboard with shelves inside for storing linens, etc. Nice Chippendale feet, but from province of Quebec. Often sold as Pennsylvania Dutch *kas*. Pine, scraped, circa 1800.
   $800

Country-made storage cupboard with shelves, or wardrobe without them. American, pine, early 1800s.
   $400

Armoire or wardrobe with two
drawers and ball feet in American
Empire style of mid-1800s. Pine
with false mahogany graining.
    $750

Gothic peak on American Empire
wardrobe—useful for restored
houses with few closets. Pine.
    $425

French Provincial armoire in
walnut, circa 1760, with cabriole
feet.
    $2,300

American Empire wardrobe of a kind often converted to cupboards. Pine.
$375

French Provincial armoire, circa 1750, with good color and carving.
$2,000

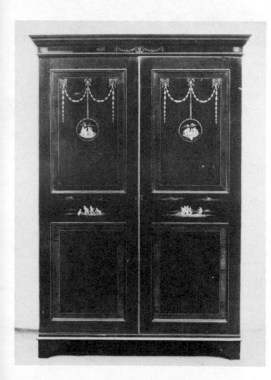

Edwardian armoire, circa 1900, painted in the manner of Angelica Kauffmann classical motifs. Basic Empire/Regency lines to case. All mahogany with satinwood inlay.
$1,500

Extra Provincial French armoire is from Louisiana. Cabriole legs, but no carving. Made in walnut and cypress. Regional collector's piece. Early 1700s.
$2,500

Small, single-door French Provincial armoire, walnut, circa 1750.
$1,450

Painted armoire of Continental origin, roughly in the French Provincial manner. Possibly Italian, mid-1700s. Worth a little less than other double-door armoires because of paint.
$1,750

WASHSTANDS

Corner washstand, circa 1760, in
Hepplewhite style. Top lifts off,
hole in subtop. Light mahogany.
$550

Sheraton gentleman's washstand,
mahogany, 1790. Stool slides
under.
$650

Two-shelf mahogany serving stand
in country Sheraton style of New
England.
$300

New York-made Hepplewhite
corner washstand with French
curve to legs. Solid mahogany.
$400

Regency into Victorian washstand
in mahogany. Circa 1840s.
$250

American Empire washstand with new top in mahogany and walnut. All stained mahogany.
$225

Mahogany washstand made in Rhode Island with label of maker. Solid mahogany, circa 1810.
$1,200

Pine washstand with new solid top to replace one with opening for washbowl. Originally painted and sold in same volume as Hitchcock and other fancy chairs during mid-1800s in U.S. However, good Sheraton lines and proportions still remain.
$175

Mahogany Sheraton-style
washstand, circa 1830. American.
$175

Washstand recently painted in a
naval manner, from England.
$250

WINE COOLERS

French Victorian walnut wine cooler. Victorian reproduction.
$650

Mahogany cellarette or wine cooler, English Regency, circa 1820.
$1,200